QUIT PLAYING SMALL

••

DAILY INSPIRATION FROM THE
CREATOR OF THE SWITCH, PIVOT
OR QUIT PODCAST

BY AHYIANA ANGEL

Mayzie Media

Mayzie Media
California
www.MayzieMedia.com

Ordering Information:
Quantity sales. Special discounts are available on quantity pur-
chases by corporations, associations, and others. For details,
contact the "Special Sales Department" at info@mayziemedia.-
com.

Quit Playing Small/ Ahyiana Angel. -- 1st ed.
ISBN 978-1-7985740-5-8

Dedicated to the loyal Switch, Pivot or Quit podcast listeners. Yes, you! You are amazing! Your willingness to explore, learn and grow is beautiful. You are appreciated and admired more than you know. You were made to shine, so keep shining!

I receive all the good that life has to offer me.

– Jen Sincero

INTRODUCTION

If you're anything like me, your parents started drilling the idea of job security and stability into your psyche from as early as you can remember. Go to school, do well in school, get a degree, find the job of your dreams, then stay there for the remainder of your career. That was stability. That was the normal way of life. That was what I call checking the boxes.

However, with exposure and access you can quickly come to understand that if you are striving for above average – for greatness – that plan won't cut it. Simply checking the boxes won't get you the results that you desire, the life that you deserve. You have to be bold, and sometimes you have to take big action! Big, sometimes ugly, often scary, rarely-in-your-comfort-zone type of action.

Our parents didn't realize that their imposed idea of security could one day create a subconscious fear of exploring unchartered territory. I'm sure they never imagined that it could cause us to hesitate when taking chances or even encourage us to think small. They never imagined that insecurity could develop, leading us to think we're not even worthy of trying.

Despite what my parents instilled in me, I've learned that it's impossible to make your mark in life if you're not willing to take chances. Consequently, if you're not willing to take chances, you may be depriving the world of the next great leader, the next billion-dollar company, or the next critical life-changing invention. One thing is for sure, you will undoubtedly be depriving the world of the best of you.

As children, we were encouraged to daydream and use our imagination. "The sky is the limit," was a regular cliché repeated to inspire us to dream big. In my progression into adulthood, I've realized that the limits established in our minds are more important than the limits of the sky. You are the only one that can hold you back by setting up perceived barriers and limitations for yourself.

When you're young, you're impressionable and naive to the existence of boundaries. You think that you can do or be anything. However, as we get older, those around us start discouraging us from thinking this way. My challenge to you is to resurrect that childlike energy, that belief that you are capable of achieving anything that you want, being whoever you want and doing amazing things.

You are craving the freedom to live out loud and do the things that you truly love daily. We all want to lead full, fabulous lives that are rich and rewarding. We want to make a great living, enjoy time with family and friends, all while having the flexibility to do the things that we desire when we want to do them, like traveling to explore faraway lands or having an extravagant meal. We want to live the lives that we've only daydreamed of, and we can do this – if we remain disciplined with reaching our personal version of success.

After interviewing dozens of women for the Switch, Pivot or Quit podcast, I've come to truly understand that success is a very personal thing. It can only really be determined by you and how you feel, anything else is just opinions from the outside world.

This is not a book about how to be the best employee or how to establish a side-hustle or how to get the courage to be an entrepreneur. It is a book that will help encourage you along your journey in identifying what works best for you and what resonates with you. It will encourage you to uncover your confidence and tap into the strength within. It will re-energize your mindset so that you are able to present yourself to the world in a way that you can be proud of. The daily entries will not only give you quality mindset tips, but they will also inspire you to take action.

Whether you are aware of it or not, the work that you do inspires others. The presence that you have inspires others. I know this now, to be able to share it with you, because of my journey. When I decided to Switch, Pivot or Quit when it came to my career and follow my heart, I had no clue that it would positively affect people that I knew, as well as those that I didn't know. I had only set out to be happy, but in the process, it encouraged others to pursue the things that they were passionate about. So although I never set out to inspire others, I eventually realized that it was a natural byproduct of my actions. That is the beauty that comes with you letting go of playing small and taking action: you inspire others.

....

OPTIMISM IS A PORTAL TO PROGRESS

When you're on your journey to greatness, optimism and an open mind go hand-in-hand. These are internal elements that can be controlled by you. Operate with the expectation that the best is intended for you and coming to you. This is the practice of thinking in favor of yourself. Training your mind to consistently think in favor of yourself may take time. It may feel selfish at first. Somewhere in our history, we were made to believe that always expecting the best is unrealistic, that cheering for yourself is wrong. Who says that cheering for yourself isn't a display of self-confidence?

There will always be a list of naysayers before you 'make it.' But don't become a part of that group, and don't engage in negative self-talk. Most days the push from you will be the biggest push that you will receive. Most people are so consumed with their own lives that they don't have the capacity to cheer you on. Adopt a practice of cheering for yourself because if you don't, how can you expect anybody else to?

....

ASK FOR WHAT YOU WANT

When you decide to quit playing small, you enter a season in your life where you just have to go for it. Otherwise, you'll wait too long, you'll think too hard, and eventually, you'll worry yourself right out of the ask. You'll come up with a variety of excuses to avoid taking action. You'll start talking yourself out of it. You'll question if you deserve it.

When playing small is no longer an option, you can't afford to talk yourself out of potential game-changers. It's go time. It is easier now to create a way for yourself where it once seemed like there was no way. There are so many opportunities available that weren't available before with the growth of the internet, smartphones, and social media.

However, you still have to speak up to nudge your way forward. Just because the opportunities are more plentiful than they once were, doesn't mean there won't be any work required on your part. You have to tap into that little bold space within yourself that says, "Okay, let me step up and ask for what I want. Let me make sure that I put myself out there and take chances. Let me make sure that I make my asks clear."

Request the promotion that you feel you deserve. Ask to meet with the person who can impact your career. Pitch to work with your dream client. Making the ask is up to you.

My first paid speaking engagement was a result of asking the organizer to be paid for my participation. Admittedly, during the conversation, I had to make an awkward segue into broaching the topic of money. At the time, I had completed a variety of speaking opportunities to build my resume, but I did not get paid for any of them. In this instance, I had leverage because the organizer approached me to participate in the conference, but I quickly realized that if I did not request compensation, it would not have been offered. I knew what I wanted, and I asked for what I deserved.

Nowadays, it is easier to connect with people that we otherwise may not know via social media platforms like Instagram and LinkedIn, but there is still a part of you that will have to step up and be bold. You may have to initiate interactions and put yourself in positions to get what you want. Although the initial stages of asking for what you want may be a little uncomfortable, keep in mind that in every situation you approach, they are still people just like you and they had to start somewhere. There may have been a time when they had to push themselves to approach someone in a similar fashion. You will not be the first, nor the last so just ask.

....

YOU CAN'T GROW WHILE BEING ANTI

Let the truth of that statement sink in. Being anti will stunt your growth as a person. It will cause you to block yourself from experiences and ultimately hold you back.

What is being anti? In the simplest form, anti is opposition. It's antagonism. It's when everything is a quick no before it is a yes. Anti-people default to a 'no' and they're routinely negative. It might seem obvious to warn you against negativity, but it's a very simple thing to overlook. It can manifest itself in so many larger ways in one's life because what it really represents is being closed off instead of being open to new opportunities and ideas.

It's challenging to straddle the line of being anti and desiring your best life. The truest way that you can embrace living your best life is by being open. Being open to everything. Being open to people, being open to possibilities, being open to experiences, being open to options, being open to what the universe is sending your way and finally, being open to saying yes more than you say no.

When you're anti, you make it difficult to receive, and you certainly cannot fully experience and enjoy your life. You limit your learning, you limit your growth and you limit your capacity for understanding. Sift through your recent experiences and identify ways in which you may be embracing anti versus openness. Make a commitment to openness so that you can expand your experiences in life and continue to grow.

....

BEFORE YOU GET WHERE YOU WANT TO BE, YOU MUST BEGIN WHERE YOU ARE

Start within, believing you can. Refuse to engage in negative self-talk. Only participate in uplifting thoughts that align with a can-do attitude. Daily affirmations are a great way to reinforce positive thoughts. When looking to elevate to your next level, it's helpful to have something to routinely lean on for reassurance.

There was a time in my life where I would have never considered using daily affirmations, not because I did not think that they would work, but because I just didn't understand their power and purpose. When I started my journey of making a Switch, Pivot or Quit, I knew I would have to develop a stronger belief in myself. As a result, I adopted a routine of reciting daily affirmations to assist me with reminding myself where I was going and why I was qualified.

It can feel a bit like wishing on a star when you first start using affirmations. Some may even think it's not useful at all, but my personal experience tells me otherwise. Just as with most things, it won't work overnight. In addition, if your attitude toward the process is negative, you'll take longer to see results from your practice.

There are plenty of suggestions and guidelines out there for creating effective affirmations. To begin, keep them simple. Affirmations should have just enough depth to speak to your ambitions, but they should also be simple enough to remember. My personal suggestion is to create affirmations with your life goals in mind. Develop a series of statements that detail things you declare to be true for your life. Be specific when developing affirmations that speak to believing in yourself and what you can accomplish.

....

CREATE, PLAN, HUSTLE, EXECUTE, AND REPEAT

Be explicit with your goals, flexible with your methods, and open-minded with your options. Building up the courage to pursue your goals or dreams can be difficult, but what's more difficult is staying stuck in your comfort zone and not even trying to pursue your dreams.

You can win big when you risk big. Pushing past your boundaries will push you past your goals.

....

IT'S EASY TO USE PLANNING AS A CRUTCH

It's a good practice to begin formulating plans before you make big decisions that will impact your
life, but you don't have to have it all planned out
to move forward. It is time to let go of hesitation,
fear, and excuses.

LIKE A FLOWER, YOU WILL BE READY TO BLOOM FULLY IN YOUR SEASON.

....

....

BELIEVING IN YOURSELF IS REALLY TESTED WHEN YOU STEP OUT OF YOUR COMFORT ZONE

There have certainly been times when I wondered if I had the stamina to make it as a creative entrepreneur — being a creative means continually creating. I often wondered if I could keep up. I had days where I would buy into limiting beliefs and question whether I'd eventually run out of ideas. But eventually as the ideas continued to flow it became clear—this is who I am. That will never change. As long as blood runs through my veins, my creativity will remain. Worrying about what could or could not happen is a waste of energy.

••

A CAUTIOUS SPIRIT IS NOT ALWAYS A BAD THING

When you are cautious, you're less likely to make hasty decisions that will negatively impact your future. You will not be careless.

Many think that in order to be fearless, you can't be cautious. Untrue: every instinct in your body was designed to help you achieve your greatness.

••

YOU GOT THIS

I know you're out there working hard chasing your dreams trying to become the best version of yourself and sometimes it feels daunting. Sometimes it seems like an uphill battle to actually get a win, but never count yourself out.

Look inside and connect with your 'why' – in other words, your purpose. Motivation is stronger when it comes from within. When you are working in your purpose wins can come at unexpected times and from unexpected places. The belief that you can pursue your goals has to come from within.

....

PERCEPTION OF SELF IS POWERFUL

What you think you're not can hold you back from greatness. What you worry that you have not accomplished can cause you not to even try. I want to share with you that it's never too late.

At some point, we start to feel like there are restrictions and timeframes put on all the areas of our lives. Unknowingly, that feeling of restrictions can paralyze you. It can make you feel helpless. It can make you feel powerless, but when you realize that it's never too late to do the things that you want to do, to say the things that you want to say, or to be the person that you want to be, you also realize you must take your power back – whether it's the power over your mind, the power over your circumstances, or the power over your own reality.

Once you realize that you can take your power back, you have to also take action.

When we're born we are conditioned to learn to do all the basics: how to walk, talk, use the bathroom independently, how to eat properly, and much more. As you grow up and go to school, you're taught another set of skills to help you learn and understand certain concepts. However, they don't teach you how to be human or navigate an adult lifestyle or figure out who you are. School doesn't teach you how to understand yourself, how to understand what you like and dislike, how to understand who you want to be, and how you want to show up in this world.

By taking your power back, you're making your life what you want it to be. At a certain point, some of us get lost and we don't really know what we're supposed to do and how we're supposed to be. In some instances, we feel powerless. We're sitting there just checking the boxes going day-to-day asking everybody what they think, what we should do, and how we should do it. We lose the ability to tap into our own genius, our own personal compass to let us know what direction we should be going in, what we should be doing, what we should be feeling, what's right for us, and what's wrong for us. In this way, we lose our power. If you really feel like you need a change in your life, if you feel stuck, if you feel complacent, I can almost guarantee you that one of the factors to your solution is taking your power back.

Owning your voice is about realizing it's not too late. It's trying the things that you want to try. It's doing the things that you want to do. It's learning who you are. It's understanding what makes you tick, because lack of understanding can breed unhappiness. We think we're happy with the things that are in front of us until we have a saddening realization that we are not and we don't really know how to figure it out. We're not properly equipped to pull back the layers and understand what's really going on with us.

When you become unhappy in your career, the days become like torture because you have to spend so much time where you work. If you're in that space right now where you're feeling a bit tortured by your day-to-day, I would encourage you to sit back and reflect on what you know for sure so that you can start tapping into self. This is especially great to do on Saturdays and Sundays when you have some alone time. Allow yourself the time to take inventory and to assess how much power you're exerting over your life. Maybe even allow yourself the time to realize how much power you're not exerting over your life and how much power you can take back to help create a life you want.

You may be thinking, "This sounds good, but my life is more complicated than that." It's like I say with everything else, you have to start somewhere. You can't look at this big change you want to make and say, "Oh I can't make those kinds of changes because it's just not feasible right now." It's still worth considering the things that you can do in the immediate future to get to where you want to be. Once you start figuring out where you think you want to be, let things continue to evolve because that could even change.

That's the beauty of life: we are made to evolve as people and professionals. No one said that by 30 years old we have to have it all figured out. You don't have to be the person that you thought you were going to be. The beauty of life is evolution. We are here to evolve. We are here to learn. We are here to experience. We are here to grow. If we weren't, our lives would end much earlier.

Fortunately, most of us will live longer than some of our ancestors due to advances in technology and medicine. The medical field is growing and expanding, constantly developing new technology to keep us alive, so why shouldn't we be growing and expanding and learning new ways to make ourselves happy while we're here?

It's never too late. It's never too late to grow. It's never too late to expand. It's never too late to change.

Yes, people may have known you as this one person. They may have expectations of you as this person. But you could show up tomorrow with your new enlightened mindset of how you actually want to show up in this world, and they'll have no choice but to accept it because that is what you decided. That is you taking your power back and showing up how you want to show up instead of how people think you should show up or how you've been conditioned to show up. You can always change how you present yourself to the world. You can also change how people treat you and how they perceive you.

It's never too late for you to take your power back and show up how you want to show up in this life. You're supposed to evolve. Don't let anyone tell you different.

....

SUCCUMBING TO THE PRESSURES OF OTHERS WILL ONLY HOLD YOU BACK

I can remember the look on people's faces when I shared my plans to leave my position in sports entertainment publicity. In some instances there was a sense of disappointment, like I had won a trophy and I was naively deciding to give it back before walking off the stage.

Of course, deciding to take a huge leap and switch careers made me uneasy. I was unsure of what my future would hold. The only thing that I knew for sure was that I had to listen to my gut, so I did. If I had fallen to the pressures of people around me who thought I had it made where I was, then I would not have taken a chance on myself. If I listened to them, I wouldn't even be writing this book.

Not succumbing to the ideas and pressures of others allowed me to soar – imagine what it will allow you to do.

....

AT SOME POINT, UNBEKNOWNST TO US, WE BECOME CONDITIONED TO FEAR

Have you noticed that a common thread in the average pursuit of happiness for humans is fear? From fear of the unknown to fear of the things that may not be good for us, fear is constantly present. By the time we're old enough to become completely aware of the fear, we start looking for ways to combat that fear. We often look to outside encouragement to break us free from the fear, but really, facing and overcoming the fear is an inside job.

The first step to overcoming deep-rooted fears is to acknowledge that they are present. When you are feeling cautious about an idea or an opportunity, take some time to write down the negatives and the positives. Under the negatives, include your reservations and your fears. You may find that identifying your fears will help you find solutions or coping techniques.

When you are equipped with knowledge, fear becomes less prevalent. Use the confidence in your talents, ideas, and expertise to shut down hesitation and timid behavior – this is rooted in fear. Successful people are often perceived as fearless. Typically that is not the case. We all have our hesitations and reservations, but those that make history do not allow fear to hold them back. They acknowledge the fear and then navigate through it. You are equipped with everything that you need to conquer your fears and accomplish your goals.

LIVE TO MAKE
YOURSELF
HAPPY. IF
PEOPLE DON'T
GET YOU,
DON'T MAKE
IT YOUR ISSUE.

13

THE REALITY OF AN AMBITIOUS PERSON'S LIFESTYLE IS THAT YOU'RE AFRAID OF BEING AN EPIC FAILURE

You feel pressure to make everyone proud, without understanding that failure is proof of progress. Most times you will not be sure about what chances to take but you take them anyway. When you are navigating through unfamiliar seas risk is par for the course and one big storm can capsize the ship of dreams that you built. Get familiar with failure and discomfort; it's the way achievers grow to the next level.

When discouraging incidents happen it's helpful to have your go-to counsel established. Although family and friends can be well-intentioned, often they don't understand how real the struggle can be for you. Network within your industry so that you can find like-minded people to communicate with over frustrations or just to bounce ideas off.

You'll need these relationships because you're going to feel alone at times, like the people closest to you don't get it, like they don't understand. Embrace their lack of understanding – because if they did get it, if they did understand completely, then it wouldn't be your journey. It would be theirs.

....

BE CONFIDENT IN YOU

You will be successful. You may not know what your success will look like; it may surpass what you can imagine. Success does not have a name on it. It will not be passed out as a prize. Success means something different to all of us, but at the core, I think you feel most successful when you know how hard you've worked for it, and you get what you've worked for.

Who you are or are not isn't what holds you back from greatness: it's your mindset that prevents you from succeeding. Confidence is your key.

15

....

NEVER LET YOUR IDEAS GET BOXED IN BY LIMITATIONS

Inspiration can come from anywhere. Remain open to the possibilities and let your ideas run free. You can never have too many ideas. When you have a great idea but hesitate to act on it, remember that if you don't do it, someone else will.

16

NO ONE JOURNEY WILL BE
THE SAME AS ANOTHER

Pace yourself through the phases of your journey. Do what you can. No business, idea, or plan will be where you want it to be overnight, and you will not be an expert in all areas when you start. But you can utilize your strengths and tackle what you can. Decide what you want, declare that you can do it, and commit to doing it. You are innovative, talented, and savvy enough to win. Multiple ideas will come and go until you find the right one. But once it hits and you reach your stride, your journey to success has officially begun.

....

WE OFTEN SEEK THE COUNSEL OF OTHERS IN MATTERS OF OUR PERSONAL AND PROFESSIONAL LIVES

When it's time to make big decisions, it feels comfortable to consult with family, colleagues, and friends. You consult with others in the hopes of lessening the feeling of confusion about your next move. You hope that someone will offer advice that will solve all your problems.

In these instances, you probably just wished that you knew what the future would hold. But let's be honest: most of us don't like being told exactly what to do. So, if there was a blueprint with each step of your life laid out for you to follow, you wouldn't follow it anyway. That would be boring and lack exploration, right?

Just keep going and keep taking chances. Taking chances can be intimidating but it is necessary to reach your full potential.

....

YOUR SUCCESS IS HER SUCCESS

It's easy to get caught up in negative self-talk and depressing comparison sessions when you see someone else winning, but what will that help you accomplish? What's for you is for you and will be yours. When you see another woman shining, help her to extend the reach of her light. Take notes and be inspired by those that are doing amazing things around you. Allow another woman's success to be motivation to let your light radiate from your soul, even if it's too bright for those around you. The illumination will attract what you need.

YOU DON'T NEED ANYONE'S PERMISSION TO WIN.

....

....

YOUR INSTINCTS WILL TAKE YOU PLACES PLANNING CAN'T

You've been optimistic about your ideas and your future. You've gone through your period of hesitation. You've encountered roadblocks that made you question whether you should keep going. Often it feels difficult to know what's 'right,' but trust your gut and you will end up exactly where you need to be.

It took three years before I finally decided to believe in my talents and give notice to my employer. Toward the end of my days as a publicist, I received back-to-back rejection letters from literary agents. Securing an agent was part of my plan to transition into another profession. I did not allow the rejections to impact my instincts, which screamed to me that my purpose was more significant than my current existence. My Switch, Pivot or Quit transition was highly intuitive. Since my initial plan was only to become a traditionally published author, eventually evolving into a podcast host and creating content that impacts thousands of ambitious women weekly was something that I could have never planned. It was merely a result of adhering to my instincts.

20

BE THE QUEEN OF KILLING IT

Let your reign be an inspiration to all. Shying away from your accomplishments when they are recognized in a public forum can seem like the socially acceptable, humble thing to do. But in your queendom, you make the rules. Kill it and clap for yourself at the same time. There is a time to be humble and a time to allow yourself to shine. Live in your moments — you've earned them.

Give yourself permission to make your own rules, live fearlessly, and be unapologetically successful.

....

BUILD A BIGGER BENCHMARK FOR SUCCESS

Growing up, I didn't know what my expectations were of myself, let alone what I needed to do to get to a point where I could call myself successful. As I continued to get older and go through life, I realized that I wasn't really reaching for a certain level of success: I was looking at the people around me and I was honestly just trying to do better than most. Maybe they were my benchmark for success. But because I only knew what they were doing on a surface level, my benchmark for success was probably a lot lower than it should have been.

Evaluate who you surround yourself with and uncover why you spend time with them. Playing small is surrounding yourself with people that you know you can one up because it makes you feel like you are accomplishing something even when you are not requiring the best out of yourself. Go bigger!

....

ALLOW YOUR LIGHT TO
SHINE FROM THE SHADOWS

People feel like they have to be timid about saying, "I don't want to be in the shadows anymore. I want to be heard. I want to be recognized. I want to do something noteworthy."

If you truly desire to emerge from the unknown place, then you deserve to be heard. You deserve for people to know about your amazing skills. You deserve for people to know what you can do. You deserve to allow your light to shine. You deserve your proverbial moment in the spotlight.

You don't want to go through life wishing you had shown up in a bigger way, wishing you had played the game of life different, wishing you had truly allowed your greatness to radiate. When you go after what you want you will activate your own unique superpowers, in the form of talents that you didn't know you had. Use them often and use them wisely. Soar!

....

WITH PLANNING, SELF-DISCIPLINE, ACTION, AND EFFORT YOU COULD BE A MILLIONAIRE

There is nothing different from you and the next millionaire to show up on the scene. Nothing is stopping you from being a millionaire. You just have to open your mind up to the possibility and do the work. You are qualified and capable.

....

SOMETIMES YOU HAVE TO THINK ABOUT YOUR JOURNEY IN TERMS OF OTHERS

Think about the people you can serve – those who can be inspired by you. Every time you have a little apprehension about your path or question your journey, remember there is a group of people out there who need you to show up as you are. Your journey and testimony may be the one thing that helps them to get on the other side of what they are facing, but you can't help them if you hide your truth.

Years from now, you may be on a stage talking about this very time: when you were not fully allowing your light to shine, when you were walking in the shadows, when you were doing the work for other people but never receiving the acknowledgment that you deserve. Despite it all, you broke through and succeeded to find your greatness on the other side.

You may be on a stage in front of thousands with a testimony of encouragement as a result of your journey, but you will not make it to that stage if you don't make up your mind that you will get out of your own way so that you can actually serve the people who are waiting to hear from you.

DON'T HOLD BACK, LET YOU BE YOU.

....

FEAR OF SUCCESS IS REAL

Fear of succeeding is not the normal conversation that one has around success, but it's real. The responsibility of being an entrepreneur, leader, independent contractor, consultant, CEO, innovator, or freelancer can be a complex road filled with ambiguity.

Despite the trepidation, you must remember that you were built for greatness. It takes little to no effort to join the crowd, but only someone special can stand out. When there is hesitation, you have to ask yourself if you really lack the confidence in your skills and abilities, or if you're actually scared to win.

....

DOING WHAT YOU ENJOY BRINGS HAPPINESS, ENJOYING WHAT YOU DO IS A DREAM COME TRUE

Identify the thing that keeps pushing you forward from day-to-day. We are not being typical and focusing on the word 'passion' because the bigger picture incorporates more elements than passion. When it's not about you, that's when you find your real purpose. When you help others flourish, you will find unbelievable success on your own path.

Where can you enhance someone else's life with your contribution? It's not always about what you're passionate about. What you're passionate about may not even be what you're good at, and your passion may not always pay you. It may motivate you, but it may not pay you. If you are looking to have a job that you are passionate about, plus pays well, understand that the two may not align.

You should also consider what you can excel at. Where can you offer the most value?

You were born as a masterpiece, and your life is a one-of-a-kind creation. Only you can determine the true value.

....

PEOPLE WILL NOT GIVE YOU WHAT YOU'RE NOT READY TO ASK FOR

There will not be a loudspeaker announcement when it's your time to seize an opportunity. That's what your gut is for.

Follow your instincts. When you've been working hard and you see an opportunity for advancement, do you wait for someone to present the opportunity to you or do you follow your gut and pitch yourself for the opportunity? You have to take the initiative. Life usually hands out subtle pushes in the right direction but it is up to you to lead the charge toward what you want. You have to be your own biggest advocate.

···

START DOING AND STOP WATCHING

One thing I learned is that you should try things that interest you. Trying out lots of different things will help you understand what works for you and what does not. If you're only observing all the time and never trying things you won't really know what you're good at. You won't really know how other people perceive you. You won't know how you're showing up. You won't know if what you're doing is working. There will always be plenty of unknowns.

Get out there anyway. You need to try things. Some will work, some will fail, but either way you will learn.

....

GIVE YOURSELF A REASON

When you get to a point where you're feeling discouraged or defeated, just remember why you started. Tap back into your why.

You're on a mission to create the kind of future that you desire. You're not in the business of letting yourself down. So forget about other people – forget about who's watching you. Forget about who you think is evaluating your wins or losses. It's not about them – it's about you not being in the business of letting you down.

During the years of producing my podcast I've been passed over for opportunities, told no and in some instances never received responses to business proposals. The disappointments don't stop me because I know why I started. My goal was to create a podcast that could inform and entertain a woman who is sitting at her work desk trying to answer the question: *what's next?* My why and the community that I serve is stronger than the impact of any rejection.

You have to keep going. You have to keep giving it your all. You have to keep being the best you can be, especially if you know that you have more in you to offer. Give everything your all and one hundred percent even when nobody's looking. Even when you don't think that people will know how much effort you put in. It's those moments where you'll be surprised that somebody else is actually looking, cheering for you and waiting for you to rise.

30

MASTER YOUR CORE SKILLS
AND HONE YOUR STRENGTHS

Put your skills and strengths on display whenever possible so that people can size you up. In this case, it's a good thing. You want them to get to know you and your strengths. You want to be known for a specific skill set. People need to understand how to consume you. They need to know what to do with you because if they don't know what to do with you, they do nothing.

During my college years, I never took the time to asses my core skills. It wasn't until I'd been in my career for some years that I realized what I was skilled at doing. I knew how to string words together in an attractive, marketing savvy way. I could use those skills to my advantage. I loved creative writing. As a publicist, you have to write materials all of the time including headlines, talking points, press releases and more. Once my colleagues started buzzing about my ability to write catchy, creative marketing copy I became the go-to person for the creative copy. My skillset became an asset.

BE ON THE
HUNT FOR
WHO YOU'VE
NOT YET
BECOME – IT'S
THE BEST
MISSION EVER.

·······································

WHEN VENTURING OUT TO DO SOMETHING FOREIGN AND ACCOMPLISH GREATNESS THERE WILL ALWAYS BE UNCERTAINTY

Uncertainty can cause you to question yourself. If you're second guessing your plans and wondering if you can really achieve the lofty goals that you set forth, you're not alone. Whether it be the little voice in your head or the chatter of others, you're not feeling as confident as you once felt and that's normal. That's fear trying to overpower your thoughts and force you to alter your plans, maybe even quit. Don't. Use your internal strength to block out fear and keep going.

....

DO WHAT YOU CAN

It's okay to slow down. Slowing down is not about completely relieving yourself of ambition, but rather reminding yourself that it's okay to allow yourself time to do what you can. You don't have to act like you are bionic woman. You don't have to put extreme pressure on yourself to accomplish a myriad of things in one day, in one week or in one month. You can overcomplicate your process and make it seem overwhelming when you put pressure on yourself to figure it all out immediately.

This beautiful thing called life is ever evolving. Only a small percentage of people have it all figured out completely and live stress-free. The majority are feeling their way through daily, constantly learning and striving to accomplish things that are on their list.

One of the keys to making progress toward your aspirations and goals is to break your challenges down into smaller pieces so that you can tackle them. The constant daily pressures that you put on yourself can cause you to actually get stuck versus make progress. Have you ever had so much on your plate to do only to look up at the end of the day having completed nothing significant? It can be production paralysis: everything that you have to do is so overwhelming and potentially intimidating that you stall and produce nothing. You don't move any closer to your goals or achieving the things that you wanted to achieve.

For example, when you look at a mountain, it might seem too high to climb. You might not feel like you have the skills or equipment to climb that mountain. You look up and it seems impossible. From your perspective on the ground, the mountain may as well be touching the sky. It's a hundred times bigger than you, and full of sharp edges and obstacles. You can't possibly see how you can climb that mountain in front of you.

Then you remember: it's okay to pace yourself. Focus on the things that absolutely require your immediate attention while you are on the ground, like learning the fundamentals of rock climbing, acquiring the survival tools you need, and identifying the gear required before you even need to think about getting to the top. You learn, you prep, you step, and you go – and before you know it you're using your skills to actually climb that monstrous mountain. You got started by using what you learned as a toddler: put one foot in front of the other.

You're not stuck trying to figure out how to climb the entire mountain anymore: you're in motion. You're working with what you have and doing the work based on what you know.

When you need to, take it slowly. Just make sure that you are achieving your personal minimum requirement. Don't try to achieve everything in your days. Just something. You might just surprise yourself.

....

33

BEING PATIENT AND ESTABLISHING YOUR VALUE CREATES OPTIONS

Your time will come. You want to see immediate results. You want things to happen quickly. I get it, but patience and persistence speak volumes. Keep giving it your all. Keep going above and beyond. You're not only establishing a pattern of excellence, you're developing your personal brand. You are establishing how people will view you and what you bring to the table, whether you're working in a corporate environment or as a freelancer.

You want to try your best to be as consistent as possible. You are establishing your value, which will then give you the options that you need to continue to excel and make your life bigger and better. The goal is for you to be the best that you can be.

Those who are watching notice the detail and the effort that you put in. They notice the time that you take to execute. They observe your capacity to go above and beyond, and that's when they really become impressed. That's when you've managed to say "I'm here" without having to say a word. Your work says: I show up and I perform with excellence every single time, so you want me on your team. That's how you want people to feel about you. You want them to want you on their team. You want them to want to work with you. You want them to value your intelligence, your expertise, and your opinions. You want to be an asset.

When you find it hard to be patient, think back to some of the little things that have gone in your favor – unexpected, but appreciated things that helped you on your journey. Those things are confirmation to keep going. That's confirmation that great things are on the horizon if you just keep being true to yourself and your talent. Your journey will continue to surprise you and it will continue to give you the little winks that you need to keep going.

34

···

YOU NEVER KNOW WHO IS TRYING TO SEE HOW YOU MOVE

Being underestimated is discouraging. You can feel like you have no energy to keep going. That's when you ask yourself: what's my motivation?

Your motivation can be a multitude of things. Maybe you want to be the best in your field, maybe you want to thrive, maybe you want to make your family proud or maybe you want to continuously rise to the top. Whatever the source of your motivation, keep doing the best that you are capable of doing. Have faith in yourself and your capabilities.

Bet on yourself, knowing that one day all of your hard work and your efforts will pay off. It may not be the day that you think it'll pay off. It

66

may be an unexpected time. It may be in unexpected ways. However, when you keep going you open yourself up to positive possibilities. You're not leaving it all to chance. You're putting everything that you have out there on the line so that it can be received by the universe.

I'm not saying any of this will happen overnight, but what I am saying is keep going, keep going, keep going. You never know who's watching. You never know who's observing you. You never know who is trying to see how you move. They may be setting up a plan to approach you with an awesome opportunity. You don't know, but if you slack off I can assure you that you'll never know.

When I was contacted to conduct a professional development workshop at Google, I had to reread the email because I thought it was spam. I didn't know anyone at Google to vouch for me. I had not pitched anyone for this opportunity, yet there it was sitting in my inbox. What I didn't know was that while I had been consistently producing my podcast weekly for the last two years, a woman working at Google had been listening and setting up a plan to approach me with an awesome opportunity.

....

MAKE YOURSELF
NOTEWORTHY WITH A NICHE

Carving out a niche for yourself in business is a great way to stand out and ensure that your presence is valued. Skill paired with personal traits can equal a unique combination that can't be duplicated. Your niche can also directly reflect your personal brand.

For example, maybe you're efficient at compiling research, and because of your charming personality, you're also stellar at presenting your research in meetings. You have two skills that you can marry together with efficient researching and stellar presenting to create a niche for yourself. Most people are not equally exceptional in both areas.

Take time to create a list of your skills and make sure that you let them work in your favor.

....

SOMETIMES WE FEAR CHANGE, BUT NO CHANGE EQUALS NO PROGRESS

Change happens daily, from minor changes to the dramatic changes. It's all a part of the cycle of life. Sometimes we fear change, but no change equals no progress. Change is inescapable, but growth is voluntary. Your attitude toward change is everything. So the good thing about change is that you can have control depending on how you choose to respond to the change.

OUR CHOICES
CREATE OUR
STORY. DON'T
LET THE
CIRCUMSTANCES
OF LIFE CHOOSE
FOR YOU.

••

....

IT CAN BE SIMPLE TO STAND OUT

Whether you're just starting out in your career or a seasoned vet in the game, the simple things can make you stand out in a cluttered world where everyone is doing their best to play big. Playing big does not always mean grand gestures. You can use strategy and the long game to play big and achieve the desired results. I'll share a few tips that I've learned to utilize:

Under-promise and over-deliver

This is a phrase you'll often hear in the business world. It's worth remembering this piece of advice when it comes to managing your clients' expectations. You should also think of your employer as a client that is paying for your service.

With that said, if you know that you can do something very well, don't oversell it to the client before the job is done. Just do it! This is where knowing your strengths and using them comes in. Do an awesome job and let the work speak for itself. If by some chance you don't perform as well as you anticipated, then your lack of cocky boasting spares you from having to tuck your tail in shame.

On the other hand, if you deliver amazing work then you just made yourself look like a star. By doing your job well, you'll pave the way for bigger opportunities.

Respond promptly

Nothing frustrates people more than having to wait on a much-needed response. Being the type of person that is always quick to respond with relevant and accurate information creates a positive perception with everyone that has interactions with you. This easily ties into building a favorable reputation for yourself. People love when they are working with someone who is responsive. It also aids in speeding up overall productivity.

Send emails as if the president of the company will read it

Yes, mistakes do happen. However, if you reread an email before hitting send you are likely to catch simple mistakes. A quick once-over can save you some embarrassment. It can also save you from peer scrutiny as a result of constant careless errors. Compose and send every email as if a senior executive will read it and take it into a high-level meeting to be shared.

Be respectful of others' time

This seems basic and almost elementary, but it is still a problem for many people. If you set a meeting with colleagues, be on time. If you know that you are running behind, be courteous enough to inform the other party. Leaving someone waiting screams that you do not respect their time. It can make them feel as though you think they have nothing better to do aside from wait around for you. This might not be your intention, but actions speak volumes, and your unintentional actions could hinder future opportunities.

....

GO FOR IT

It's easy to get caught up in the day-to-day tasks that weigh you down, but the goals that linger in the back of your mind are there for a reason. It's never too late to set time aside to chase your dream. Try that business idea, bid for the promotion, take the certification class or anything else you've thought about doing. You will never regret trying, only never attempting to see what your best could be.

Go for it. Don't wait!

....

BE BOLD

I know, it might seem easy for me to say. Just the thought of taking a risk makes you start shakin' in your boots. But it's time.

I can share this with you because I've had to tell myself the same thing even when I was fearful of what it would mean. Being bold is something that requires you to tap into an inner strength: a strength that helps you to do what once felt impossible. If you have a dream to fulfill and you want to be great, it's time to mix up your actions and get bold.

If you're not sure how to be bold, start with asking for what you want. Resign to being aggressive with going after your goals. You don't have to change the character of who you are to be bold, just recognize where you can step it up a notch and take action. Trust that it is for your greater good and you will not regret it.

....

YOU WILL BREATHE GREATER LIFE INTO YOUR DREAMS IF YOU CELEBRATE EVERY TINY VICTORY

Often we put so much stress and pressure on ourselves to win the big wins that we overlook the little wins and accomplishments. They count too. Chasing your goals daily can feel daunting at times. Some days can seem horrid, and you might feel like nothing is going your way. Then there are the days when the stars align and things seem like they're falling into place.

Even if the things that fall into place aren't life-changing, we must get in the practice of celebrating every tiny victory. Celebrating your victories is a form of gratitude – and gratitude draws in positivity. The more that you can keep yourself operating from a positive headspace, the more that you can have a clear head when moving forward. There are so many potential things that can devastate us in this world, so why not celebrate the things that uplift us?

···

IF YOU PLANT A SEED,
GROWTH IS INEVITABLE

Make sure that you sow and nurture what you
want to grow. What you put out into the universe,
either conscious or unconscious, can potentially
manifest into something real.

I know that some people give a major side-eye
to manifestation. I wasn't convinced either until I
realized that I had unintentionally manifested my
first traditional book publishing deal.

It started with planting the seeds. For nine
months, I woke up an hour early before work every
morning to write. In the evenings, if I wasn't working on my manuscript, I was researching how to
become a traditionally published author. Self-publishing was an option at this time, but it wasn't as
popular as it is now. A few people even mentioned

self-publishing as an option for me, but I quickly shut down their suggestions with my truth: "I'm going the traditional route." Although I did not have any connections in the publishing industry and I was a first-time author, I had planted the seeds and convinced myself that I was going to be a traditionally published author. I can remember saying that every traditional publishing house would have to turn me down in order for me to even consider self-publishing. I had nothing against self-publishing, but securing a spot with a publisher was my only goal.

I didn't intend to manifest anything at the time, but my mindset was positive. I never had thoughts of not getting published. I was dedicated to my goal and confident that it was something I could achieve. I strongly believed in myself and I wasn't looking for validation from anyone else. Within four months of finalizing my manuscript, the seed that I had planted blossomed. I was offered a contract to publish my book through an imprint of one of the top publishing houses. Looking back, I realized that what made my experience happen was the fact that I had decided what I wanted. I planted seeds to allow my dream to take shape and

I got not only what I manifested but also what I
worked for.

....

FEAR IS EXPECTED BUT QUITTING IS NOT AN OPTION

You will have your moments where you ask yourself, "am I doing the right things? Am I making the right decisions? Should I give up? Is my timing right?" This is when you start having doubts about everything. You're scared that somewhere along the line maybe you made the wrong move.

But think about it: when you're growing up and getting ready for the world at large, people rarely talk about facing the inevitable, doubting yourself. They don't show you how to combat those feelings. Rarely will you get a tutorial on how to face the fear of believing in yourself. As a result, at a certain point in your life as you start to encounter some of these things you realize that it's really up to you to figure out how you're going to navigate.

Identify ways to cope. Energize yourself to build yourself up to face the doubt and the fear.

One of the things that I know to be extremely important along your journey is having a good circle of support around you. When things get tough and you are challenged by different situations, having a supportive circle that truly believes in you does wonders to lift you up. You don't always need the smartest or most accomplished people in your circle. Look for the selfless people who are genuine, honest, and caring as well as good listeners. They will help you confirm what you already know: greatness lies within you. Prosperity, awesomeness, and favor lie ahead in your future.

This core group will help you handle what comes your way. If you think about quitting they will remind you why you started. If you feel defeated, they will lift you up. They want to see you win. And that's what you need when you're trying to respect and honor your greatness because it's not always easy.

You have to shift your mindset when doubt starts to creep in and the times where you start to feel fearful. You have to remind yourself of your special gifts. You are in this situation for a reason.

Because you can do it. Because you can handle it. Because you are meant to be great. You are meant to move from the present and flourish.

Quitting isn't your only option. Instead, trust your community to lift you up.

TO BE FEARFUL IS TO EXIST. TO BE FEARLESS IS TO LIVE.

****

....

TODAY IS THE DAY THAT YOU ARE GIVEN

You have the ability to make choices and decisions as to how you want to proceed in this life. What will you do to ensure that you are working toward your greatness? What opportunities will you look to create for yourself? Today is the day to take charge of the controllable elements in your life.

Some circumstances can't be changed. But that is not what you will focus on. You can only focus on the things that you can change. Some of us tend to put things off as a result of fear, laziness or any other excuse.

Today is no more significant than any other day, but today is the day that you can make a choice to change behaviors, chase your dreams and do more to ensure that you are giving 100% toward achieving your greatness. Let's do it!

....

KINDNESS IS A TOOL THAT MOST DON'T RECOGNIZE AND MANY OFTEN UNDERESTIMATE

I try to make it a point to treat everyone kind that I come in contact with because I learned early on in my career that the gatekeepers are often the people that you least expect.

When you treat people with kindness, they remember it. Kindness is free so dish it out regularly. Throw out compliments, give away smiles, do little things that will make someone's day. This world can be so overwhelming for many. The kindness that you give can be the difference between a good day or a bad day for someone. For you, it can be the difference between signing that new deal or not even getting called back.

....

LEARN TO SHIFT TO A SOLUTION-ORIENTED MINDSET WHEN YOU FACE CHALLENGES

Don't let your vision for your future be obstructed by obstacles. Unforeseen challenges can always pop up so rather than spend energy on feeling defeated, channel that energy into overcoming. When an obstacle comes up, you should immediately ask yourself, "how can I navigate around this?"

You never know your true strength until you are tested, back against the wall. That's when you really see what you're made of, what you can create, and what you can accomplish. The successful person looks at a challenge and embraces the challenge.

Once you embrace the challenge and refuse to spend your energy fighting it, you will be able to think with a clear mind and plot your next steps. Your next steps may turn out to be your best steps and your most cherished opportunities.

....

EMBRACE THE BEAUTY OF BEING UNIQUE

Despite being created to be unique – from personality to fingerprints – most of us eventually conform to an idea of sameness. Standing out makes you different, and in your youth, that feels like a disaster. We all longed to blend in as children. However, different can be good when it comes to making your mark in life and business. Different can give you an absolute advantage. Hold on to what makes you unique – it's your strength.

I encourage you to embrace the beauty of being unique, of being different. Think different, be different, move different – it's easier than trying to blend in because it feels authentic. Explore the opportunity of being unique. Your path is uniquely your path, so allow yourself to roam.

....

YOU CAN NEVER HOPE TOO MUCH

Desiring an amazing life is rational, but living your life without acknowledging your desire is unreasonable. You can never dream too much. Dreams create a desire in your heart. Without a desire for something more, greater or bigger, our lives would not be as rich.

Be a dreamer, but a doer as well. You may not always fulfill all of your dreams on the first try, but that does not mean that you shouldn't try. The only regret that you will know is the regret of letting a dream go. Don't stop dreaming!

....

IT TAKES A WISE PERSON TO REALIZE THAT THEY ARE NOT YET WHO THEY HAVE THE POTENTIAL TO BE

When you're young, it's not such a hard thing to accept. However, as you get older you feel this societal pressure like you should have everything figured out. You feel like there are goals you should have met, people you should know, and places you should have seen. The truth is that despite your place in life most people feel this way because life is a journey and not a destination.

The reality is that it takes time, awareness and growth to identify the type of person that you want to be – let alone actually go through the steps necessary to become that person. Take your time and let your life be lived.

YOU'LL NEVER
KNOW IF YOU
CAN BALANCE
ON THE
TIGHTROPE OF
SUCCESS IF YOU
DON'T CONQUER
YOUR FEAR OF
HEIGHTS.

••

....

A NEW DAY BRINGS NEW OPPORTUNITIES AND POSSIBILITIES

When you're very ambitious, it's commonplace to let the days fly by and the little moments slip past you. You keep looking ahead, preparing for the next day to conquer and the next task to demolish. When that's your reality, it's easy to forget to take the time to look around you and observe the present. Acknowledge what you have accomplished along the way to where you want to be.

This is a little reminder to give yourself a break and take it all in by being present. You will regret not being present in the moments that will be the foundation of your future. You will not get the moments back no matter how much you make or how much you spend so enjoy them.

....

THE BEST DON'T GET IT RIGHT FROM THE START; THEY START TO GET IT RIGHT

A winner knows loss. A winner knows struggle. The struggle is like a rite of passage, so stop trying to skip it.

We all want to avoid struggling. However, most success stories involve points of adversity and struggle. You rarely hear someone saying that their journey was an easy ride. Here's a thought: maybe the quicker you embrace the struggle and work through it, the quicker you will come out on the other side living in your absolute greatness! The struggle just may be the necessary stepping stone.

....

IF YOU DON'T STOP FEAR, FEAR WILL STOP YOU

Fear can be sneaky. It can trick you and disguise itself as excuses. It can mirror obstacles that get in your way. Fear will whisper that you already have too much on your plate. Fear will shout that you don't have time. Fear will make you feel intimidated by everyone who is more qualified than you. But it's your job to stop fear in its tracks. Shut it down with confidence so that it does not stop you from achieving greatness. A confident mind is not easily intimidated.

I encourage you so passionately because I'm not a stranger to fear and what it can do. Staying in a career that I was no longer happy with was fear. Waiting so long to take a chance on me was fear. Letting the roar of others drown out my voice was fear. Not wanting to step in the light and shine was fear. Always being so humble was fear. I'm proud to say that now I'm finally going hard in the direction of my purpose and there is nothing or nobody, myself included, that can stop me.

I have not mastered fear, but I have mastered the art of pushing myself. Push yourself toward the things that make your stomach uneasy at the thought. You will survive. Push yourself toward doing the things that make you feel shy. You will survive. Push yourself toward the things that make you want to turn away and run. You will survive. How do I know for sure? Because I am a daily survivor of fear and you can be too.

52

•••

OWN IT IN POWER

To own your voice you don't have to be the loudest; you just have to stand firm in your words. Have truth in what you speak, integrity in your delivery and passion in your prose. The world may try to twist your words. The world may try to convince you to change your words. These are things that all powerful people must endure. You will be tested because to play big, you must take ownership of your voice. Say what you mean, and mean what you say.

....

YOU CAN STOP TRYING TO PAINT THE PERFECT PICTURE

Your life can be similar to a work of art. Let the beauty of natural, unaltered moments create a masterpiece.

The canvas is blank when you are a baby. Colors, textures and tones are added as you begin to explore and learn from your environment. Artists are not limited in what their art can be. You are not limited in what your life can be. Some elements are intentional in creation and some accidental because creating art is fluid. Let your life imitate art, allow it to turn into your greatest masterpiece.

....

NEVER GET TOO COMFORTABLE

Whether you have a 9 to 5 or hustle hard chasing checks as an entrepreneur, having a game plan for your life is the foundation for conquering your goals. Things will change, you will change, and your plan may change. Pivots may be necessary but plans are a great way to help you embrace a pivot. When the plan is not working, rework the plan.

A plan does not have to be rigid with pages of details. It can be a summary of your vision. It can consist of elements like ambitions, time frames, roles, benchmarks, and goals. For example, your game plan can consist of things like attaining a specific professional status, ideas for career advancement, an intention for growth, or hell – even a vision for world domination! Only you know what you want the future to hold for you. So I challenge you to spend some time thinking about your vision.

YOU WERE
BORN INTO
FREEDOM –
DON'T LET
YOUR DREAMS
LIVE IN
CAPTIVITY.

··

NOTHING AND NO-ONE SHOULD BE ABLE TO MAKE YOU IGNORE YOUR INTUITION

Your intuition is that feeling that you have inside. That little voice, your gut, your instinct, whatever you would like to call it. Just don't call it wrong. Learning to follow your intuition is the best gift you can give yourself.

If you pay attention, you will eventually find that when you listen to your instincts, they do not lead you wrong. It can be challenging to make some of the decisions that you'll face, but we all experience those challenges so you're not alone.

If every minute of our lives had already been laid out, and we knew exactly what was going to happen from minute to minute, what would be the point in living? There would be no excitement, no mystery, no spontaneity, no variety, and certainly no room for you to listen to your intuition.

Just a little reminder that you have the answers, everything that you need is inside of you. You will not steer yourself wrong.

....

TAKING A RISK ON YOU REQUIRES ZERO DOWN PAYMENT

Not taking the risk, though, could cost you every-thing you ever dreamed of.

....

SIMPLICITY SUCCEEDS

Some days can be long, exciting, hectic and the people and things in them command so much of your attention. It can be overwhelming, but when you simplify things in your life it brings clarity. You can see what really needs your attention. You can see what requires your action.

If you're feeling overwhelmed and don't know where to start, I can tell you that I always start with what is within my control. For example, declutter your room, set aside clothes that you want to get rid of, clear off your desk, clean out your makeup drawer, or tidy up your computer desktop. These things will not drastically change your life, but they can help you take control and streamline. Remember, we are trying to simplify to eventually reach a place of clarity so in this process you can start with the simplest actions.

....

SURROUND YOURSELF WITH PEOPLE WHO WANT TO SEE YOU WIN

Are you surrounded by people with the best intentions?

As life happens, your support system is crucial. When things get difficult, it's empowering to know that you have a team of people behind you rooting for you to win – not secretly waiting for you to fall or fail.

I'd rather have supportive strangers around me than fake friends any day!

With that in mind, be keenly aware of who you share your *big* goals and plans with. Share it with people you can turn to when you need that extra push to open that boutique, ask for that promotion, go on that date, take that trip alone. Whatev-

er your heart desires, you can do it. Just keep people around you who actually believe that you can
do it too.

••

59

YOUR MIND WILL BELIEVE EVERYTHING YOU TELL IT

We are filled with an immense amount of power before we even understand the depth of it and how to really tap into our power.

The complexity of a mind can have you riding high, believing that you can conquer the world one day and slumped on the couch dreading life the next. We can take ourselves through a range of emotions within a limited time frame. The realities of the human brain and it's power in action. So what will you do with all of that power? Determining how you will manage the power within you requires an awareness that it exists. People often talk about mindset because it truly matters and it is an element of your being that is well within your control. Developing the awareness to train and retrain your mindset to interpret things in a way that is most healthy for your existence is a powerful tool. It may not always be easy, but you control your mindset which interprets your reality and allows you to react.

Don't underestimate your power to impact your reality. Think about what you want. Envision what you want. Know that what you want is possible. Understand that what you desire is within your reach and act as though you already have what you desire. You have the power to expand your mind and what you think is possible for your future so that you can make it a reality. Embrace limitless possibilities!

60

....

YOUR DESIRES DESERVE
TRUTH

While sitting with a friend at brunch talking about ambitions and careers, I realized how much we tend to not be truthful with ourselves. Even among trusted friends sometimes we still find it hard to declare our true desires. It can be for many reasons but number one is usually fear: fear that what we desire may come true and fear that it may not. Mind-boggling, I know. We can also want something and fear getting it all at the same time.

My friend went on to make a comment that indicated she straddled the line between wanting to be recognized in her industry as an authority and at the same time not wanting to seek attention. This is what we call playing small.

Unfortunately, you can't have it both ways. You have to be decisive with your desires. Otherwise, you are sending mixed messages. How can the universe (or anyone else) help you to get what you want if you are not clear? Say what you really want and speak up for what you want. How many times have you verbalized your desires to other people, yet downplayed the role that you really want to play? How much of this is due to you not thinking that you can achieve said desire, or not feeling worthy of thinking that you can? That's not helpful, it's hurtful. But it will help you hurt your chances of getting what you want.

I followed up on my friend's declaration of her desire and asked a pointed question: "Do you want to be recognized for your talents or not?" She hesitated for a brief second, then promptly said yes with conviction. Her expression seemed a little relieved to have finally admitted what she truly wanted.

It's okay to admit what you really want. Share your real desires in truth moments with friends. Allow yourself to hear your truth, and feel it as well. Clearly verbalizing your desires makes a stronger case for making your desires a reality.

DON'T SEEK APPROVAL, SEEK INSPIRATION.

··

....

61

CREATE YOUR OWN OPPORTUNITIES

You are not limited to what someone else will give you. When you realize that you will not get what you need to advance your agenda, it is up to you to brainstorm actions that will allow you to create an opportunity for yourself. Let's say that you were passed over to work on a new big project at work. Okay, now it's up to you to think of a bigger and better project to pitch and incorporate yourself as the lead. Maybe you didn't get selected as a speaker for this big industry conference that you've been dreaming of attending. That's fine. Create your own plan to launch an appealing conference of your own and give yourself top billing. You get the idea. If it is not happening for you then there is nothing stopping you from creating what you want to be a part of.

After I signed the contract with my publisher to release my debut book, I was naturally excited. I was so sure that they would be planning a big multi-city publicity tour for me with media mentions secured from coast to coast. I was very unfamiliar with the book publishing industry so I didn't know that my daydreams of a fabulous book tour would remain a fantasy if I left it up to my publisher.

I quickly found out that the press department was stretched thin and the only way that they would ever plan a promotional book tour for me was if I had somehow become a noteworthy celebrity overnight. I was feeling disappointed and defeated even before the book was launched. It didn't take long for me to acknowledge my reality, digest my feelings, and come up with a genius idea: I would create my own book tour!

In the weeks leading up to my book release, I researched venues in cities where I had friends that I could stay with. I ordered advance copies of books. I selected special gold Sharpies to scribble my signature in each copy. I locked in locations, booked flights, contacted book stores, created mailing lists, developed flyers, and most importantly, used all of my resources to create an opportunity to showcase my new book in seven U.S. cities. I was proud of my accomplishment in writing a book, but if left up to my publisher my newest achievement would have only been a drop in the bucket of books launched during that time. I had to create my own opportunity to shine.

As a result, I sold more copies, rallied people around my project, got interviews on local morning shows and created a buzz.

People will not always give you what you want, but nobody says that you can't create what you need.

....

YOU RADIATE GREATNESS

Just because people haven't recognized your greatness, doesn't mean that it's not there.

Be the best you. You don't require validation nor approval. Seeking it will only let you down. You may not realize it, but you could easily be seeking the approval of someone who is busy seeking the approval of someone else. The people that will value you and praise you most are those who are confident with their position in life. When someone is preoccupied with reaching their own greatness, any hint of yours may be too much for them. Don't take it personally – we are all human and prone to selfish feelings.

Some of the most talented people in history were dismissed and overlooked by peers, gatekeepers, industries and would-be fans early in their careers.

Stefani Germanotta, known professionally as Lady Gaga, is a great example. She began playing piano as a child, took acting classes and even signed to Def Jam records for her vocal talents only to be dropped months later. She kept going and making music. Eventually, she signed with Interscope Records but still had an uphill battle. Radio stations told her that her music was too "racy," "dance-oriented," and "underground" for the mainstream market. Her debut album, *The Fame*, went on to break industry records with sales and win her a Grammy Award.

Think about this: like a great artist, maybe your greatness is too advanced for your timing. It does not diminish the value, it only slows the recognition.

....

THERE IS OPPORTUNITY ALL AROUND YOU IF YOU CHOOSE TO SEE IT

Be the master of your mind. How you choose to interpret circumstances and react in situations can turn a rejection into a victory. Stay committed to trying to find the light.

....

YOU CAN WORK ON ACCOMPLISHING ANYTHING YOUR HEART DESIRES

When I started exploring my own ideas and trying to find out what truly worked for me, people thought I was crazy. I had disregarded others' expectations. I did not fit their mold. And that's okay.

The beauty in deciding to be free is that you don't feel compelled to meet their standards, answer their questions, or live the life they approve of. Getting to that space is a process, though. It starts with digging deep to uncover the internal confidence in you, the confidence that will guide you through. You got this boo!

....

A FOCUS ON PERFECTION WILL DISTRACT YOU FROM YOUR JOURNEY TO BEING YOUR BEST

You will never start if the prerequisite is perfection. You will be distracted by what you don't know and cannot do.

Perfection is a prison and fearlessness is your key.

Admittedly, I've never been a perfectionist and sometimes that felt bad, like I was an underachiever or my expectations of myself were not high enough. However, as I've experienced life and seen how there are certainly other factors tied with the expectation of perfection from oneself, I feel relief. Perfection is a heavy burden to carry.

If you are looking to achieve greatness in life, your validation for your achievements won't come wrapped in perfection. You have to get out and try and fail and learn and try again because that brings advancement, experience, and understanding. Perfection brings excuses and paralysis. Be free.

....

STOP HOLDING YOURSELF BACK

How many times have you talked yourself out of what once seemed like a brilliant idea? Decided that you were not qualified before even applying? Sat mute during a crucial conversation even when you had great value to add?

From big to small, we all manage to find ways to hold ourselves back and often we don't even recognize it. I know I've held myself back when I walk away from the situation and I think about what I should have said or how I should have acted or what I should have done.

Stop holding yourself back!

BEING SHY
WILL LET
OPPORTUNITIES
PASS YOU BY. BE
BOLD AND SEIZE
THEM WHILE
THEY'RE LOOKING
YOU STRAIGHT IN
THE EYE.

....

....

GET HONEST WITH YOURSELF

Being honest with yourself requires more out of you and your awareness. So often we allow ourselves a pass, but this is you taking a real good look at yourself and making a concerted effort to develop into the person that you really want to be. Think of the things that you do that may allow you to play small and assess the why behind those things. Quit playing small when it comes to getting honest with yourself by identifying your areas for improvement or areas where you're lacking and need to be better. Once you identify those areas, do something about it. You take action by holding yourself accountable.

Ask yourself questions daily that will challenge you. Think along the lines of: what do I need to do to show up for myself? How can I play bigger?

How can I be a better version of myself? What's one thing that I can do to step it up today? It's not a one-time thing. It's a daily activity to check in with yourself to get honest with yourself.

··

TAKE ADVANTAGE OF BEING UNKNOWN AND USE IT AS A SECRET POWER

When you're not yet well-known, you'll face less judgment and fewer expectations. In an age where everyone wants to be seen, let obscurity be your training ground. This is your time to develop your skills, try out your ideas, learn what you don't know, make mistakes, learn from your mistakes, try again, and get better. Eventually, you will be ready for the grand stage.

Imagine that you are to give a televised speech to an audience of millions. You lobbied hardcore for this huge opportunity because you wanted to prove yourself. Now that you're backstage, your brow is sweating profusely, and you haven't even laid eyes on the audience yet. Your stomach feels nauseous. Your legs are unstable like noodles. Your mouth is suddenly dry. You wanted this though. You wanted to shine. You walk out onto the stage facing the blinding bright lights. You can hear your own heartbeat thumping through your chest. You keep saying to yourself, "This is your big chance, don't mess it up." Then it hits you, you've never read from a teleprompter before and that's what's staring you dead in your face to help you deliver your speech. This is typically a position that only a seasoned professional would be in, so of course nobody backstage thought to ask if you're familiar with a teleprompter. Of course you are, you're a professional!

The first few words start scrolling on the screen and in a matter of seconds you fumble trying to spit out a basic word in front of the millions watching. Your mortified face is now worthy of a meme.

Wouldn't it have been better if your first experience with a teleprompter were on a local level where maybe only a few dozen people watched you fumble? Take advantage of obscurity while it lasts.

....

BE GENTLE WITH YOURSELF

Be gentle with yourself, you're learning the ways of a woman.

Be gentle with yourself, you're learning the ways of the world.

Be gentle with yourself, your mind is unmatched.

Be gentle with yourself, your passion is unparalleled.

Be gentle with yourself, you've transformed into a woman from a girl.

70

....

BE AWARE OF WHO YOU ALLOW TO TAP INTO YOUR LIGHT

You are dynamic, talented and powerful just by being you. The more that you grow personally and professionally, the more that others will be drawn to you. Some people will simply want to better understand what they are attracted to, and others will want an opportunity to dissect how you do what you do. Assess carefully who you want to grant access to. Access can fill you up or it can be draining for you.

....

SOMETIMES YOU'LL FIND YOURSELF HOLDING ON TO WHAT'S FAMILIAR BUT NO LONGER SERVING YOU, BECAUSE IT'S JUST THAT: FAMILIAR

You'll find yourself consistently staying in a space that you know invites average into your world. Is average working for you or do you want more?

You have to know when to let go and open yourself up to the challenge of change and greater possibilities. A key indicator is comfort. Do you do the same thing daily because you like it, or because it's comfortable?

....

YOUR LIFE ISN'T A RACE TO THE FINISH LINE

During the course of your career, the location of your finish line may move and the length of time that it will take to get to the desired point may also change. People who successfully reach what they wanted to achieve always advise enjoying the journey – because you will inevitably get to the finish line but you can never recreate those fundamental moments.

Things to consider: Did you take in the sights and sounds when the lessons were learned? Did you allow yourself time to value the skills you developed and experiences that were given to you as a result of your journey? Did you develop unbreakable relationships with colleagues? Were you present?

Through your day-to-day experiences, the journey won't always feel enjoyable. You may feel anxious because you want to reach your goal – you want to be the best and you want to prove to your peers that you are the best. You want to be valued in your industry. It's understandable if you feel that way, but if you don't regularly check in on yourself, those feelings allow the comparison game to creep into your psyche. Comparing your accomplishments to your peers. Comparing your life to those you see only online. You can enjoy the journey more when you remove comparison.

You are you for a reason. You are learning the lessons meant for you. You are gaining the knowledge meant for you. You are growing into the individual that you are meant to be. There is no race to become the best version of you. Nobody can beat you at becoming the best you.

Keep looking straight ahead and go at your pace.

DO SOMETHING TODAY THAT CHALLENGES YOUR LIMITS.

....

MAKE MOVES

When you want to move forward but hesitation and fear creep in, my advice is to do it anyway. Take it one action, one step, one move at a time. The pieces will come together. You're only a failure if you allow yourself to buy into the narrative that convinces you not to try. Nobody can be the judge and jury over what makes you a success or a failure, only you can. The biggest failure is in never trying.

··

BECOMING A GAME CHANGER MAY NOT REQUIRE WHAT YOU THINK

It may be as simple as you infusing your natural gifts into the game. They always say that there is nothing new under the sun and I believe that's true. However, your rotation on this earth is unique. It's never been done before. The unique character of our fingerprints is proof that you were designed to be one-of-a-kind. Use that to your advantage. You don't always have to be the first ever to change the game. Be innovative with adding in your personal touch and the gifts that come naturally to you. Avoid overthinking it and let your best flow. The little details often make the difference.

....

SERVING OTHERS SERVES YOU

When you take yourself and your interests out of the equation and act from a place of selflessness, sometimes you stumble upon what you actually needed. Operating from a place of service to others not only builds goodwill, it can also create options.

....

OTHER PEOPLE QUITTING ON YOU DOES NOT MARK THE END

When everything is changing and you're questioning all that you know, take comfort in the fact that you won't let yourself down. Create opportunities for yourself. Get creative and keep going.

....

PEOPLE SEE YOU

People often see you better than you see yourself. They see your work, they see your drive, they see your dedication, and they see your consistency. Observing how you present consistently allows an ally to assess where you need help. Even when you don't see it, there are always people watching you and rooting for you to win. They will appear when you least expect it to offer a connection, lend a hand, or give you an opportunity. Their generosity will not be a result of pity, but because you've worked for it.

••

SUCCESS DOES NOT HAVE A NAME ON IT

Success means something different to all of us, but at the core, we feel most successful when our accomplishments align with our goals.

It used to feel like success was reserved for a select few. Only special people could achieve success.

Now, I feel successful daily because I embrace all of my accomplishments and allow them equal impact on my life. Once, during an interview for an article, the writer asked me to name some of my accomplishments and state which ones made me proud. I have learned to appreciate everything that I have accomplished, so I read off a laundry list of accomplishments from graduating college to moving to London because those were all times when I felt successful.

The meaning of success is personal. Own your wins. Be proud of yourself, girl!

SUCCESS DOES
NOT REQUIRE
AN AUDIENCE
TO ITS RESULTS,
IT DRAWS AN
AUDIENCE TO
ITS RESULTS.

....

79

....

YOU WERE CREATED FOR GREATNESS, DEVELOPED WITH A PURPOSE, AND DESTINED TO SUCCEED IN EVERYTHING YOU AIM TO ACHIEVE

You are intelligent and resourceful enough to use obstacles to motivate you. You will triumph. Walk in expectation that you will get what you work for. Adopt an internal attitude of entitlement to success. You deserve what you allow your thoughts to manifest. When you bet on yourself, the odds are always in your favor. Step from behind your fears daily to enable yourself to take action toward your dreams. Be courageous when in search of the sparks that will set your soul on fire. Be unapologetic about your desire to achieve your goals. Make moves each day, big or small, to place yourself in a position to be one step closer to your destination of greatness. It doesn't matter how many people do what you do, nobody can do it quite like you.

....

LET THE DESIRES OF YOUR SOUL SPEAK TO YOU

Give yourself permission to do what stimulates your spirit. Developing an understanding of self is not easy, but required to listen to the desires of your soul.

Recite to yourself:

Being positive can result in me achieving amazing things in my life. I believe that anything is possible. I can do hard things. I am determined to keep growing and winning. I am intelligent, resourceful and resilient. I am worthy of success and wealth. I choose greatness over fear.

....

YOU'RE NEVER TOO MUCH,
YOU'RE ALWAYS ENOUGH

Insecurities in others can manifest themselves in ways that cause them to project their insecurities and shortcomings onto you. Don't believe the hype.

You will always be too much of something for somebody at different points in life. That's okay though; you were not created to blend in or be for everyone. The beauty and fullness that you have inside of you cannot be contained or drowned out by the insecurities that float among us.

Your unique characteristics create your person. When you shrink your person to accommodate others, you're killing off a little piece of you because somewhere deep inside you are creating the narrative that whatever you're shrinking is unacceptable or uncool. It could be your quick wit, your vibrant attire, your boisterous laugh or your mild manner. Show up and let your full person exude, despite what the norms may be.

Don't believe it when they tell you that you're too much and never speak twice to a person who tells you that you're not enough. You're just enough of everything that you were made to be, and you're too much of everything that someone else wishes they were.

....

WHAT WILL YOUR LEGACY BE

How will you be remembered? How will people speak of you when you are no longer here?

I started thinking about legacy when I found out that a friend unexpectedly passed away. He was in his thirties and unfortunately fell victim to a fatal car accident. It was devastating, but the first thought that gave me a glimpse of happiness was how he lived.

We met on vacation while sipping slushy margaritas on Miami Beach. We became fast friends, and I quickly realized he was the type of friend you always wanted around because things were just better when he was in the mix.

He lived a good life. He lived a life filled with joy. A life filled with self-expression. A life filled with travel and unlimited good times. He made so many extraordinary memories in his life that although his life ended way too soon, the one thing that I could take comfort in was that he lived a full life in his short amount of time with us on Earth.

Nothing is promised to you. You don't know what will happen to you and how things will take shape in your life from one day to the next.

If you were gone too soon, how would you want your loved ones to remember you? What do you want your legacy to be? The imprint that you leave on this world matters.

It's easy to sideline the things that you really want to do or achieve because you think there will always be tomorrow. You delay developing into the person that you really want to be because you think you have time. You say to yourself, "I have too much going on. I can't think about this right now." You decide that you'll work on yourself next week, but that time never comes. This narrative of *one day soon I will do it* becomes repetitive, so much so that it makes you feel good to simply think about it and make plans in your head to do it without ever intending to take action. Your dreams won't expire, but your time on this earth will.

If you want to be the person you've always dreamed of being, or live the life you've dreamed of living, then at a certain point you have to hold yourself accountable. Stop giving yourself a pass because you don't know what's ahead for you. Start creating your ultimate legacy today so that when your days are done and you're nothing but a memory, that memory will reflect you being the best person that you wanted to be.

It's up to you how people remember you. When you are gone, your opportunity to share your greatness with the world dies with you. How would you feel if all of the great things that you know you want to do remained inside of you because you didn't give yourself the opportunity to shine? How would you feel if you knew that you didn't push hard enough to get your greatness out into the world? You may have a really dynamic, life-changing thing for this world to experience but we won't get the opportunity to experience it if you keep putting it off.

You say to yourself: I'll work on it tomorrow. Life often gets in the way, but I ask you again: what do you want to be remembered for? It is totally up to you. Take time to reflect on what you've done in your life up until this point. Consider the type of life you've created for yourself and if there are things that you want to amend.

You don't have an infinite amount of time and you don't know when the time on your clock will stop. So maximize the time that you do have. Make the best of your time, make the most of your time and live this life to the fullest. Give it everything that you've got.

....

INDULGE IN YOUR INTUITION

When my personal development journey began I hadn't even realized that self-help was an industry. At that time I could count on one hand how many self-help books I had read. As a result, my development process wasn't in accordance with a book, a coach or a program. I simply did things that felt right. I focused on things that seemed like a good idea for me to try, explore, or look into.

First, I knew that I needed to get out there and get myself involved in the activities that interested me. I was exploring *me*. I was exploring my likes and my dislikes. I was exploring what type of life I wanted to live and what types of things I wanted to see present in that life. Eventually, I did everything from taking acting classes to flying trapeze lessons. I immersed myself in anything that would open my mind to things that I hadn't thought of before. I sought out situations that would potentially make me uncomfortable and cause me to grow. That was me following my instincts, that was me following my intuition. I wasn't following a designated plan or self-help guide. I share this because it was a part of my journey and not because those tools can't be helpful. However, I will caution that you can cloud your mind by consuming so much information that you eventually don't know what feels genuinely right for you anymore.

On your journey, allow yourself to tap into your inner compass. It will lead you to what feels right for you and good to you. You can't look at someone else and think they're going to give you the complete guide for your journey. The key is that this is your journey. If someone else understood every nuance and how to guide you through all the twists and turns of your journey then it wouldn't be your journey, it would be their journey.

Uncertainty will always be there. You won't always know what to do next, how to move, or what's right. Just follow your intuition.

....

INITIALLY, YOUR BEST TALENTS MAY BE OVERLOOKED BY YOU

When you are in the process of learning and be-coming the woman that you want to be, you have to choose yourself first. It's up to you to experi-ence life in a way that feels in alignment with your truest self, but figuring that out can be a journey. Every day, you learn more about who you are and how you want to be treated in this world. You learn what you like and dislike, what you prefer, and what you can do without. You also learn a lot more about expectations – you'll learn that you have to let them go sometimes.

I find it so beautiful that in the midst of becom-ing your ideal self, you're also learning to go inside and love yourself. That's what choosing you over everything is all about. When you truly love yourself, your light can't be dimmed. Your shield of goodness can't be penetrated. Your core is not easily shaken. You develop an internal confidence that's unmatched when you choose you over everything.

Although you're working towards being a better woman every day, just remember to give yourself a break during your discovery because this is a process. This is the stuff that they don't teach us: that real-life emotional and personal evolution shit. A superhero may not know her power until her time of need – give your powers time to reveal themselves.

SOMETIMES YOU HAVE TO BLOCK OUT AND BOSS UP.

••

....

WHEN YOU ARE LOOKING INTO EMBARKING ON A NEW PROFESSIONAL ADVENTURE, IT'S EASY FOR DOUBT TO CREEP IN

You begin to wonder if you are qualified. You may question your abilities and let doubt talk you out of what may be good for you.

Let's uncover what it looks like when you are uncertain of yourself: You have hesitation in making a move. You downplay your presence. You forget about your accomplishments and let fear lead. You shy away from sharing your content with others. You question your qualifications. You concern yourself with what others will think. You let go of what you know and allow yourself to feel unqualified.

Somewhere along this journey, you became accustomed to asking for permission – not just permission to do the things that you want, but also permission to be the person that you want to be. I see so many people seeking permission that they don't need before making a significant move in life. Give yourself permission to believe in yourself. Be confident that you are qualified and be determined to try.

When your days get quiet and you're sitting somewhere reflecting on your life, it won't matter what people thought nor how qualified they thought *you* were. If it won't matter then, don't let it matter now. What matters is how you commit to contributing your skills to this world.

With technology at our fingertips, there are so many unconventional careers and business opportunities available to us. The internet has created access and opportunity. You can get a degree or certifications online. You can teach yourself new skills or how to solve a problem via YouTube. You can start a lucrative business from behind a laptop in your living room. You can start a movement with the push of a publish button. You can dream up any future that your thoughts will allow.

It's all up to you. Don't wait around for someone else to validate you, your qualifications, or your skills. You know what your qualifications are. You know what your skills are. You know what your talent level is. It's up to you to go out there and show the rest of the world what you do, how you do it and what you bring to the table. You only have one life to live so make it great. Success depends on the second letter in the word and that is you.

....

YOU HAVE TO BE WILLING TO BE SEEN TO BE SUCCESSFUL

If you're feeling frustrated by where you are or the role that you're playing, a part of the frustration may be attributed to being terrified of being seen.

Are you terrified of being seen? If you think about it, how many of us routinely operate from a hidden space, intimidated at the thought of being seen, noticed or observed?

It's often a comfortable space because being seen requires you to live up to expectations, to deliver, and to operate at your best. It opens you up to judgment. Most of us do not want to be judged, and that's why we run from it. When you fly under the radar you can get away with doing average things and being average. You can get away with putting in little to no effort. You can get away with not being your best. You are less likely to be judged. But if you want big results, you have to put in big effort. You have to push fear aside daily to show up as the best version of yourself.

••

EXTREME PRESSURE EITHER EXPOSES WEAKNESS OR MAGNIFIES STRENGTH

When one thing doesn't work out, it feels like everything is doomed to fail. But it won't.

When life gives you an error message, remember that you still have your power supply. Reboot and keep going. Tap into your why when you feel discouraged. It's easy to feel defeated by the smaller elements of your circumstances, but keep the bigger picture of success in mind. Disappointment is temporary, but quitting impacts you for a lifetime. You're not cut from the cloth of a quitter, so never give up.

··

YOU ARE BEST SERVED WHEN YOU STAY TRUE TO YOUR CHARACTER AS OPPOSED TO WHO YOU WANT PEOPLE TO THINK YOU ARE

Hiding any aspect of yourself may cause you to diminish your natural appeal.

As a child, you were fearless. Your mind was free. However, society and the people closest to you shut you down and make you feel like you need to be fearful of certain things, including yourself. You can end up feeling like you need to be aware of yourself in an insecure way, not showing up as your authentic self.

When I think back I can probably pinpoint where I was shut down and told to act, be, or feel a certain way – a way which was not in line with who I was growing into. I remember crying very easily as an adolescent when I had to talk to my parents about something of significance. If I was getting chastised or I needed to express my feelings about something, tears would almost certainly overwhelm me. I remember my dad asking why I was crying. He would easily conclude that there was nothing to cry about. But obviously if I felt the need to cry, then to me, there was something to cry about! That was a part of who I was. Constantly hearing this voice questioning my emotions made me start to reconsider how I really should feel. It made me start to feel like maybe I was doing something wrong. Maybe I shouldn't be me. So, in a sense, that contributed to me not letting the true traits of my personality flourish and grow for a long time.

Was there ever a time when you had to shut down some of your true emotions or characteristics out of fear of judgment? One of the things that you can do to get back to your truest self is be honest. In the past you may have been knowingly or unknowingly trying to fit into a mold. That is the way that the world grooms you. You learn to do things to blend in.

Now it's time to unlearn those adopted behaviors and make a conscious effort to relearn your true, dope, and authentic self. Learn what makes you happy. Learn which environments let you thrive. Learn how you respond in certain situations. In my case, for example, I know that in certain situations I am prone to tears. That is a part of me learning myself. Once you truly learn yourself you can then learn how to use your characteristics to your advantage. Make the skills, quirks, and perks of your personality work for you.

....

WINS SHOULD NOT BE TAKEN TO THE HEAD; LOSSES SHOULD NOT BE TAKEN TO HEART

If you're on a mission to be great, when you fall, get back up and get back to it. Missteps are proof of progress. Believing in yourself can't stop in the midst of challenge, that's when it starts. You may encounter your greatest success just after your most devastating failure. You won't get credit for your failures, but collect them like war wounds for show-and-tell when you finally reach the spotlight.

....

ONLY YOU CAN DEFINE WHAT IS POSSIBLE FOR YOU

Measure your success against your capabilities. Are there areas in your life where you are only giving minimal effort, and you know deep down that you could be giving more?

If the answer is no, you're on track. You are right where you are supposed to be. Don't beat yourself up for doing your best. On the other hand, if the answer is yes, if you know deep down that you are capable of producing greater, then you need to step it up. Period. You are capable of more so show up every day and in every situation with that in mind! Show up like you care. Give one hundred and ten percent just to make sure.

After you have consistently given your all to any area of your life where you knew that you could stand to improve, see how you feel. You will feel pride because you showed up for yourself and produced in a way that you knew you were capable of. Many people want the results and not the work, but what they fail to realize is that operating at maximum capacity will cause you to avoid muddling through mediocrity. Be your best.

A CAUTIOUS MIND CAN BE THE BIGGEST DREAM KILLER.

••

....

WHEN YOU SET OUT TO PLAY BIG YOU DECIDE THAT YOU WANT TO WIN

I can think back to times in my career where I wasn't showing up to play big and as a result, I wasn't winning. I was showing up to fit a mold. I was showing up so that I wouldn't be intimidating. I was showing up so that I would check the boxes. I was showing up in all these different ways that were not necessarily being authentic and true to me. I wasn't showing up to win, I was showing up to say that I was there.

In my personal life, my personality was big and confident. However, that confidence wasn't coming through in my professional life because I had not committed to winning. I was existing. As a result, I got to a point where I felt like I needed to break out of my life. I felt like I was a woman caged. I was ready to pull those bars apart with all of my might, stretch them to either side, and bust out of the professional prison I felt locked in.

I know now that I felt locked in because I was not honoring what was in line with my person. Why? Because I had not taken the time to understand my person and commit to giving her what she needed to thrive. I was giving her what I thought everyone else wanted her to have. There was no longevity in that path and it would never foster feelings in me that made it imperative that I give my all to win!

The world will not benefit from you hiding your dopeness so don't deny it, don't downplay it, and don't hold it back. Own your magic and nurture it. It's easy to get caught up in the day-to-day and overlook the little things that make you special, but remember, that's your winning magic.

....

START TELLING YOURSELF YES AND APPROVING OF YOURSELF MORE THAN YOU DISAPPROVE OF YOURSELF AND TELL YOURSELF NO

Negative self-talk can creep into your subconscious and eventually overpower your thoughts daily. It's difficult to recognize when it's happening because it's like a constant reminder in your head to bet against yourself. It's the scroll in big red letters on the Jumbotron in your mind that says, "Someone else can do it better than you, so why should you even try?"

By telling yourself yes you're saying that you believe in you. That's powerful because it takes courage. You may have to stand in the face of adversity, but you believe in you. You may have to endure being told no repeatedly, but you believe in you. You may have to sell yourself to a room full of doubters, but you believe in you. Your approval of self will make anything that you do more convincing.

....

BE EXCLUSIVE WITH YOUR IDEAS

Not everyone will cheer for you. When you have a new idea you get excited. You want to share with friends and family. In some cases, you may even look to validate your idea among your peers. I encourage you to share your ideas. Sharing can be the gateway to making your idea a reality by way of someone offering a connection, an introduction or even a monetary investment.

However, be mindful when sharing and follow your instincts. You know who the people are around you that are prone to be negative about everything. You also know who routinely cheers for you, even when it comes to the little things. Share with that person. People don't mean to be a downer when it comes to your dreams but sometimes your big dreams scare them. Sometimes your big dreams are a reminder of what they're not doing.

....

IN SOME INSTANCES YOU CAN KNOW TOO MUCH

Naivety has a negative connotation. However, I think it's okay to be naive in some instances. It may even prove beneficial. The ambition of the naive will trump the trepidation of the seasoned.

For example, when you don't know how challenging a situation is said to be or how hard a certification is to pass, you can go into it with the full confidence of a winner. The potential challenges are unknown to you so you won't agonize over them. You won't walk into the situation feeling defeated because of what you've heard. You will prepare for the challenge, face the challenge and succeed because you did not have a chance to bet against yourself before the challenge even started.

....

DISCIPLINE IS A KEY COMPONENT IN TRANSFORMING FROM AVERAGE TO EXCEPTIONAL

Goals are great, but you should look at them as a starting point. They are the markers along your journey but the real success lies in the action. When you're clear about your goals and design the plans to achieve them, your success becomes intentional. Discipline is what carries you over the finish line.

You can read as many books as your heart desires on any topic that you think will better equip you for your future, but if you do not retain the knowledge from said books and have the discipline to apply said knowledge, you are simply an informed person with little to show for the information that you've consumed. You want to be an informed person who took their goals and turned them into action, took their knowledge and applied it to create success. This takes discipline.

Success does not depend on what you know, but rather how you use what you know.

....

YOUR STRENGTH LIES IN YOUR RESILIENCE, YOUR DISCIPLINE, AND YOUR WILL

Three powerful words that are best adopted as descriptive traits when you are developing yourself into your best. I'll break down what each term represents when you quit playing small:

Resilience: Returning to form after being pushed, pulled or bent in different directions intended to break you.

Discipline: Your ability to stick to a routine or regimen that develops or improves a skill or outcome.

Will: Your drive to keep going. The control that your mind has over its actions.

Growing to the next level in your life will test you. It will require you to tap into aspects of your person that you may not have explored yet. The above traits, whether utilized alone or together, will help you become a better professional. Tap into every asset in your personal arsenal. You will need them all to be at your best.

IF YOU LIVED A LIFE WITHOUT REWARD, YOU PROBABLY LIVED A LIFE WITHOUT RISK.

••

....

THE DREAM IN YOUR HEART WOULDN'T EXIST IF YOU WERE NOT EQUIPPED TO FULFILL IT

Life will continuously place demands on you, but the biggest demand will be to follow your heart. What matters is what you believe you can do and what you put forth the effort to do. Prove yourself right! Do it despite the odds and never underestimate the moves you make, they matter.

•••

INTENTION IS GOOD, BUT ACTION IS EVEN BETTER

Action will always beat intention. Many people have the best intentions but most of us will never know because we could not see it in their actions.

Intentions don't win awards. Intentions don't earn promotions. Intentions don't make history. So don't be pacified with intentions, demand results.

....

YOU CAN'T GO INTO A NEW SEASON EXPECTING TO BRING THE OLD WITH YOU AND WIN

Don't be timid about where you are going or ashamed about the aspirations that you have for where you want to go. Be brave in your declarations for yourself. Let go of old habits, old ways of thinking, old rules, old expectations, old mindsets and anything else that does not fit the winning ways of your new season.

If you've been preparing for your winning season then you knew that the time would come when you had to let go. Letting go of what you know can feel like a challenge, but I choose to look at it as an invitation to do better.

....

INVEST IN YOURSELF

Many of us look for change but often miss the opportunities right in front of us that can help usher in that change. Why? Because the opportunities come dressed in work and dollar signs. They require investment from us – investment of our time or investment of our money – and that can sometimes feel like too much.

You look at how much something will cost or require and feel intimidated by the investment. Investing in your personal or professional growth means that you have to show up for you in a larger, more significant way. The thought of doing so can easily spark a narrative of excuses: *I don't have enough time. I need to use that money for something else. I just don't have the means.* All of the excuses are rattled off freely.

Instead, we must be solution-oriented. All of those things may be true, but do you want to stay where you are or do you want to see movement? If you want to see movement, you need to find a way to make those investments possible. When you really want something, you find a way to make it happen.

Everything that we do is a conscious decision to invest in one personal fund or another. It could be the travel fund, the fashion fund, the lavish dinner fund, the new car fund and on and on. Even though it may not feel like it day-to-day, every dollar that you spend is an investment and you have the power to decide how you invest in you.

As a society, we are quick to invest in impressing others with material things, whether that be a house, car, clothes, trips, and so on. The real test is: can you show up for yourself? Can you impress yourself? Can you sacrifice enough to quit playing small so that you can invest in your personal or professional development?

I've had to make hard decisions about whether to invest in something that I needed to advance myself or something that I wanted to just enjoy myself. During a work trip in Miami, I received yet another rejection email from a literary agent stating that he liked the storyline of my book but he could not shop it around to his publishing contacts without the proper editing. I felt crushed. I started to wonder if my dream was really meant to be. Then I reread his email and realized that the solution was staring me right in my face: I needed to get my manuscript professionally edited so that agents like him could actually take my work serious and shop it around to publishers.

Just after leaving my corporate gig, I had a tough decision to make. With no other job lined up and only having my savings to rely on, would I take a chance and invest thousands in myself to get my manuscript professionally edited, or would I keep going as I was, shopping around a project that lacked editing and cross my fingers hoping for better results? I had to ask myself: how bad do you want it? I spoke to my father about my dilemma and he asked me a very straightforward question: "How much do you believe in this project?" I answered that I knew I could get it traditionally published and that I truly believed in myself. His response, "Then spend the money and get the editing done."

So that's what I did. I invested in myself and it was one of the best decisions that I made. As a result, when I had my next opportunity for my manuscript to be reviewed by someone influential in the publishing industry, I was ready. Four months later I had a book publishing contract in my hand and that same editor that I hired was the first person that I called with the good news.

So now I'm asking you: how bad do you want it? How bad do you want to quit playing small? Lastly, what are you willing to sacrifice?

....

REALIZING THAT SOMEONE OUT THERE BELIEVES IN YOU AND TRUSTS YOUR VISION MORE THAN YOU DO IS A SCARY REALITY

Sometimes it feels like they believe harder than you do. And this might be a fact, because maybe they can see a light in you that is convincing them of your potential. Maybe they see a talent in you that they know will continue to flourish.

Don't question why they believe in you, rather glean off of their positive energy and use it to fuel yourself. Make it a daily priority to work on the manipulation of your mind to believe in yourself just as much as your supporters do. It takes awareness to alter long-standing thoughts of lack and inadequacy. Most of us don't intentionally doubt ourselves, but somewhere along the line it becomes routine, and then eventually we start to believe it. Appreciate those around you who believe in you, because they are your lifeline to experiencing personal triumph.

....

NEVER LET YOUR DREAMS HIDE BEHIND THE INSECURITIES OF OTHERS

Your aspirations can eclipse their fears. You don't have time to take ownership of feelings that are not your own.

It's astonishing what you can accomplish when you're not worried about making mistakes or impressing those who are watching. You are able to think freely and act without hesitation. When you resign to the fact that all of the greats made mistakes, and that some even operated in fear, you can welcome your faults and celebrate your missteps because they are evidence of progress. You are operating in your fullness when you are living, learning, trying and doing.

Don't let your life be guided by a soundtrack of fear. Let the melodies of chance, optimism, and courage be all that you hear.

SURROUND
YOURSELF WITH
PEOPLE FREE
FROM THE
POISON OF
PESSIMISM,
NEGATIVITY CAN
BE CONTAGIOUS.

....

....

IT'S OKAY TO BE SELFISH WHEN IT COMES TO DEVELOPING WHAT'S BEST FOR YOUR FUTURE SELF

There is a stigma against selfishness because we think that it is saying you prioritize yourself over others, and it is, but in the case of your future, you should!

You are your number one priority. Working on making yourself better will inevitably benefit those around you as well. Take note of who you allow access to your space and time. If they don't want better for themselves how can they want better for you? Surround yourself with people that under-stand that because they've done or are doing their own personal work. And when you start to notice your growth, you will also notice that everyone can't grow with you.

Quit playing small with the people that you surround yourself with. It is said that one of the biggest success hacks is surrounding yourself with the right people: like-minded people. Your circle should consist of people who are at varying degrees of outward success. Those who have accomplished above-average results, those who have accomplished amazing results, and those who have accomplished results out of the stratosphere.

Exposing yourself to different levels of accomplishment will offer you different advantages and insights. Position yourself to be surrounded by the best.

....

REVISIT YOUR ACCOMPLISHMENTS IN UNCERTAIN TIMES

This action will reignite positive energy. It will remind you of what you are capable of as well as boost your confidence. When you walk in confidence, your fears will be overshadowed and your presence felt. The competition will not be a factor. A confident mind will dull the noise of competition, rejection, and failure. You will always have to persistently participate in the manifestation of your future.

....

WHEN YOU'RE CLEAR ABOUT YOUR GOALS AND DESIGN THE PLANS TO ACHIEVE THEM, YOUR SUCCESS BECOMES INTENTIONAL

Behind every goal accomplished was a vision and the will to try. The rush from accomplishing a goal and overcoming fear is addictive. Seek it out. Enjoy it. Then get used to it.

....

NEVER LET THE FEAR OF THE UNKNOWN CAUSE YOU TO WITHDRAW FROM YOUR DREAMS

Life is limitless when you begin facing your fears. If you haven't found your success, it may be hidden behind your fears. Clear your mind of fear and doubt, they won't ever help you out. Fear is contagious. Let go of fears that detour you, hold on to ambitions that guide you. How much are you willing to pay for fear, it can cost you everything.

··

SMALL THINKING ELICITS SMALL REWARDS

If you want greater your thoughts have to be major. What you say will be. What you think will be. We all have doubts, don't let your doubts scream louder than your dreams. Make your vision so clear that your doubts become insignificant. Doubts are normal; they will always be there. Just don't embrace the doubts and allow them to take up valuable space in your mind when that territory could be used for strategically planning big wins.

Big wins call for you to exceed expectations. Interrupt apprehension with boldness. Work on making yourself proud, everything else will fall into place.

··

WHAT SEEMS CHALLENGING NOW WILL ONE DAY BE YOUR DRESS REHEARSAL

In my experience, practice does not make perfect – it makes a professional. Your pride may be bruised a bit when you struggle and your ego may be smashed when you encounter a loss but struggles reveal strength and even bad days give you something, experience. Life can draw you back to propel you into something amazing.

After experiencing my very first termination from a job, I had no clue what my next step would be. I had moved to New York less than six months before this, and everyone in my life quickly began to ask when I would be moving back to California. I was frustrated by their question. It felt like they didn't believe in me. It felt like they were kicking me when I was down. They didn't ask this question to be disrespectful – it was rather a projection of their own fears. They expected that I would play it safe and run back to the comforts of home in California.

Of course, I didn't do what was expected! I chose to stay in New York. I chose to continue my love affair with a city that I had only newly gotten acquainted with, but I knew that I loved. I survived on pennies a month after paying rent, bills, and standard living expenses. I could not afford to stay, but I was determined to at least try. My circumstances didn't stop me from appreciating the ability to roam the streets of the city, have new experiences on my meager budget, and meet new people.

However, in time, I still found myself behind on my student loans, robbing Peter to pay Paul, and desperately thinking of ways to hustle to earn extra cash. I was taking meetings with people, zipping through the city, and trying to stay positive. It was a rough time, mentally. There were definitely moments when I questioned my path and where it was going. I did not know what was coming my way but I knew that I wasn't ready to give up.

For six months I barely scraped by. Then finally, favor shined its light on me and I got the call. Well actually, I got two calls: a major record label and a major sports league both wanted to hire me. I went from being destitute to having options.

It may feel challenging in the moment, but finding the good in situations is the best way to bounce back. Respect the pace you're working at and remember life is like a science experiment: it gets good and interesting when shit blows up.

BEING
PERSISTENT CAN
OPEN
OTHERWISE
CLOSED DOORS,
BUT BE
PREPARED TO
PUSH.

....

DON'T LET YOUR PAST DISCOURAGE YOUR PRESENT

You never fail; you only succeed in finding out what doesn't work. Always remember that you're talented, competent, and fearless even when it feels like you're not. Be future-focused, have a vision, but don't rush progress. Keep going, you're worth it, your dreams are worth it.

Greatness is a daily battle between who you know you to be and who you are growing to be, play to win.

....

THE IMPACT OF YOUR FUTURE SUCCESS WILL BE FAR GREATER THAN THE IMPACT OF YOUR PAST SHORTCOMINGS

One day you won't recall the struggle you thought would last forever. Once you have success, you'll wear your failures like a badge of honor.

....

WHEN TALENT IS GIVEN TO YOU, RECEIVE IT WITH A GRATEFUL HEART AND A TENACIOUS SPIRIT

Second-guessing your skills is like being ungrateful to the universe.

Appreciate your talents. Use your talents to do things that will add value to your life and the lives of others. When you find a team that believes in your talent and helps you execute your dreams, reciprocate the vibe and uplift them as your tribe.

....

NO ENDEAVOR IS EVER A WASTE OF TIME, IF IT DIDN'T RESULT IN WHAT YOU WANTED, IT RESULTED IN WHAT YOU NEEDED

You may not get it right every time, but it's more important that you tried. Don't dwell in defeat – relish in possibility. Let your emotions be independent of your present circumstances. If you allow them to, mistakes can mold you to be the best.

....

TODAY'S REALITY BEGAN AS YESTERDAY'S DREAM, SO START NOW

When you look at the achievements of some of the best it's hard to envision what their start must have looked like, but every expert was once an amateur. The best thing that you could ever do is believe in yourself and trust your gut. If you have an idea, try it out. If you have a desire, go for it. Each day we are given an opportunity to try or try again. Visualize yourself making a living doing what you enjoy, hold the vision close, and don't let it go until it's a reality.

....

BEING FORCED TO WAIT ON YOUR TIME TO COME CAN BE AN AMAZING OPPORTUNITY

Many admittedly want oven-baked results while using microwave tactics. In order to enjoy the juicy flavor of a freshly baked dish you have to allow time to prepare the dish, let it bubble to perfection in its juices and finally, let it stand so that the dish can settle. Think of your process in the same way. You may feel every itch in your soul compelling you to rush what you desire but don't give in – use your will to wait.

Waiting allows you time to observe. You can dissect the processes, hone your skills, create alternative approaches, develop innovative solutions, and finally master your craft – all while patiently waiting for your time to rise. When it is your time, you will outperform expectations and exceed anticipations because your success will be calculated. Your success will be intentional. Your win will be deliberate. Your performance will display the skills that you mastered while waiting with patience.

WE ARE GIVEN
WEALTH IN THE
FORM OF TIME.
IT'S HOW YOU
WILL SPEND
YOUR WEALTH
THAT MATTERS

●●●

••

DIALOGUE ABOUT YOUR DESIRES

Allow your thoughts to be pushed out. Out from a place that feels uncomfortable because you will remain in that state if your dreams continue to be untold. Share what moves you. Trust someone with your thoughts. The right people are around us for a reason, and sometimes it's as simple as to help us start.

....

DISTRACTIONS CAN COME DISGUISED AS OPPORTUNITIES ULTIMATELY DETOURING YOU FROM MOVING AHEAD WITH WHAT YOU KNOW YOU SHOULD BE DOING

Be mindful that every opportunity is not the best opportunity for you. It does not mean that it is bad, it just means that you have streamlined your goals and you understand your plans. Allowing this disguised opportunity to engage you will distract you from your plans.

As you continue to excel in life you will encounter these opportunities more often. People like to dress things up to sound appealing but when you pull back the layers you might realize that it does not serve you as much as it may serve them. I can recall people regularly approaching me to be a part of producing a new event or working on a great new project – but once I became extremely clear with my agenda I could easily identify the opportunities that would help me further my agenda versus those that would only cause me to delay my goals.

It can feel uncomfortable saying no the first few times. However, instead of thinking of it as saying no to them, remind yourself that you are actually saying yes to you. The clearer you get about your goals, the easier a no will just roll off your tongue.

....

DON'T FORCE IT

'It' could be a number of things, including opportunities, relationships or growth. Pay attention to the feelings that you feel. Everything has a time whether you know it or not, whether you like it or not. When you start getting down on yourself because you have not completed that project in the time frame that you wanted nor achieved that goal by the desired date, give yourself a pass. The timing may not be right. Pressure will not make it better.

I can remember wanting this job at a top PR agency so bad that I was willing to turn my life upside down to make it work. The hiring manager was demanding from the start and I felt an immense amount of pressure. Something felt like it was pulling inside of me but I did not know exactly why. I can remember asking myself if I was forcing the situation, but I quickly shoved those feelings aside and proceeded with the rapidly moving process. In a little under two weeks of giving notice to my old company, I was sitting at a new desk in a new role, and in a little over a year later I was sitting on the unemployment line waiting to collect a check after being laid off for the first time in my life.

I don't regret my decision. I learned so much. It was my first time being let go from a job and it felt humiliating initially. But after about an hour of devastation, I suddenly felt relief. From my rushed start in the position to my swift end, I was stressed all of the time. I felt like I had the weight of the world on my shoulders, but we were not curing cancer. Looking back, in my gut, I knew that I was forcing it but I did not care because I wanted the experience. However, there is always a price to pay when you force things.

I also learned that it's okay to take your time. Whenever you feel like you are being pressured into a rush decision, be wary. Anyone that has good intentions for you will not make you feel intimidated or rushed in decision making. I don't trust when someone is trying to rush me because

I've learned that the sense of urgency comes from a place that's usually not good for me, there's more than likely something that they would rather I not pick up on in haste.

If it is good for you then you will not need to force it – it will be.

118

EXTERNAL VS INTERNAL SUCCESS

I've learned so much about the topic of success through my interviews with dozens of women on my podcast. How people connect with it as well as interpret it.

The final question at the end of every interview is, "What does success mean or look like for you?" The answers have been anything but uniform. It started to make me realize that my own views on success needed to be reevaluated. I had been unconsciously holding on to an idea about success I had as a child, but I had not taken the time as an adult to understand what it means to me in the present. I solely associated success with things like achievements, money, and social status.

However, as an adult businesswoman who has encountered tremendous highs and endured her fair share of lows, I now realize that success has to be based on more. So in short, I concluded that to me, success in life is about what you feel, not what you can show. It's about how you show up for yourself, and as a result, how you feel about how you have shown up for yourself.

Despite any personal realizations, there are still societal norms that we all must contend with. Being able to show material things makes many people feel accomplished and successful – especially since we live in such a consumerist culture. Because of this, I've devised two ways that we can approach success: external success and internal success. External success closely ties your feelings of accomplishment with the elements that others can see. It's the degree, the house, the car, the fancy clothes, the professional titles, the designer labels, the luxury, the enviable lifestyle. But are you happy? Enter internal success, which is a very private feeling and sense of accomplishment. It does not have to be proven to anyone or approved of by anyone. It is not up for debate or judgment because it can only be determined by you.

So many of the women I've interviewed say that happiness is essential to their definition of success. I attribute that to their personal experiences and exploration of the idea in terms of what fits for them. I challenge you to take time and consider which version of success connects best with you?

....

119

CIRCUMSTANCES WILL NOT CHANGE UNTIL YOU DECIDE THEY WILL

Commit to quit playing small. Be confident in you.

Things are working in your favor daily. Envision a life filled with abundance. Continue to push yourself to flourish and grow. Express gratitude daily. Be open and always learning. Participate in new experiences. Do not expect perfection from yourself. Life is a learning process, so take it one day at a time.

YOU WILL
ALWAYS GROW
WHEN YOU
REACH OUTSIDE
OF THE NORMS
THAT YOU
KNOW.

....

WRITING CORNER

THE CORNER

Our technology-driven society makes simple things like writing feel archaic. We take notes in our smartphones, record ideas in the voice notes, schedule plans in the calendar app and set up reminders for every little thing, or at least I do.

I want to challenge you to spend some time indulging in a little writing corner especially for you. A place where you can continue to explore yourself, write out ideas and create a vision for things to come. The writing corner is your space to express, plan and ponder. There is freedom in writing; no limits, boundaries or judgments.

The following pages consist of quotes and writing prompts to be utilized during reading *Quit Playing Small*. Spend time alone with your words or bring the topics to a group of friends for discussion. My only hope is that you indulge in a way that feeds your spirit.

SHE COULD ONLY STOP WHEN SHE REACHED THE TOP, BUT THE SKY WAS THE LIMIT SO SHE NEVER STOPPED

Do you feel like you have limits on your potential? If yes, are they imposed by society or self-imposed?

****

EXPANSION OF YOUR KNOWLEDGE INCREASES YOUR LIKELIHOOD OF SUCCESS

List at least two books you would like to read in the next six months to help you expand your knowledge. Share why you think it will be useful for you to read each book.

****

IF YOU'RE ALIVE, CHANGE IS STILL AN OPTION

State one minor thing you can change in the coming weeks to impact the greater good of your life.

....

SIMPLICITY BRINGS CLARITY

What can you do today to simplify at least
one aspect of your life?

****

VISUALIZING YOUR GOALS IS MORE POWERFUL THAN TALKING ABOUT THEM

Allow yourself to spend at least 10 minutes per day in silence, visualizing what it would look like to achieve one of your goals. Write out your vision.

****

A FREE MIND BREAKS THROUGH INVISIBLE BARRIERS, A CLOSED MIND STOPS AT INVISIBLE ROAD BLOCKS

What's blocking you?

****

YOU WERE NOT BUILT FOR AVERAGE; GREATNESS AWAITS

When you think about yourself, what does being the greatest version of yourself look like?

****

FOLLOWING YOUR TALENTS WILL LEAD YOU TO THE RIGHT DOORWAYS OF OPPORTUNITY

List a minimum of five talents or strengths that you possess.

••

ATTEMPTING TO DO WHAT YOU THINK YOU CAN'T DO TEACHES YOU WHAT YOU CAN DO

Recall a time when you did something that you did not think you could do? How did it make you feel?

****

BEHIND EVERY SUPER WOMAN THAT YOU ADMIRE, THERE IS A SELFLESS WOMAN THAT INSPIRES

Who are your inspirations or women that you would like to model your life or career after?

••

EXCUSES WILL GET YOU EXCUSED FROM THE POSSIBILITY OF GREATNESS

What excuses are you holding on to?

****

PROCRASTINATION WILL LEAD
TO THE DEATH OF YOUR DREAMS

Write down at least five things that you will
do this week that you know you have been
putting off?

****

YOUR BEST IS YET TO COME

Write about one thing in life that you are
most looking forward to accomplishing?

****

START WITHIN, BELIEVING YOU CAN

Create a specific mantra that speaks to believing in yourself and what you can accomplish.

****

SURROUNDING YOURSELF WITH LIKE MINDS WILL CHALLENGE YOU TO GROW THROUGH YOUR STRUGGLES

Identify at least one new like-minded person that you would like to connect with and begin to befriend in the next 30 days.

****

YOU WILL ALWAYS HAVE TO PERSISTENTLY PARTICIPATE IN THE MANIFESTATION OF YOUR FUTURE

List one activity that you will participate in to manifest your future in the next three months. (i.e. vision boards, networking, coaching, workshops)

****

LIVE LIFE FEAR FREE

If you did not have any fear of failure, what would you do or try?

****

CHANGE IS INESCAPABLE, GROWTH IS VOLUNTARY

Share how you know that you have grown as a person from the you last year?

****

TODAY'S REALITY BEGAN AS YESTERDAY'S DREAM, START NOW

What is one minor thing that you can do now to start going after one of your goals?

****

ANSWER EVERY CALL THAT EXCITES YOUR SPIRIT

What makes you excited to wake up every-day?

••

DAILY JOURNALING

I am grateful for:

My affirmation for the day:

Three things I will hold myself accountable for today:

1.

2.

3.

Today I accomplished:

I am grateful for:

My affirmation for the day:

Three things I will hold myself accountable
for today:

1.

2.

3.

Today I accomplished:

I am grateful for:

My affirmation for the day:

Three things I will hold myself accountable
for today:

1.

2.

3.

Today I accomplished:

I am grateful for:

My affirmation for the day:

Three things I will hold myself accountable for today:

1.

2.

3.

Today I accomplished:

I am grateful for:

My affirmation for the day:

Three things I will hold myself accountable
for today:

1.

2.

3.

Today I accomplished:

I am grateful for:

My affirmation for the day:

Three things I will hold myself accountable
for today:

1.

2.

3.

Today I accomplished:

I am grateful for:

My affirmation for the day:

Three things I will hold myself accountable
for today:

1.

2.

3.

Today I accomplished:

I am grateful for:

My affirmation for the day:

Three things I will hold myself accountable
for today:

1.

2.

3.

Today I accomplished:

I am grateful for:

My affirmation for the day:

Three things I will hold myself accountable for today:

1.

2.

3.

Today I accomplished:

I am grateful for:

My affirmation for the day:

Three things I will hold myself accountable
for today:

1.

2.

3.

Today I accomplished:

I am grateful for:

My affirmation for the day:

Three things I will hold myself accountable for today:

1.

2.

3.

Today I accomplished:

I am grateful for:

My affirmation for the day:

Three things I will hold myself accountable for today:

1.

2.

3.

Today I accomplished:

I am grateful for:

My affirmation for the day:

Three things I will hold myself accountable
for today:

1.

2.

3.

Today I accomplished:

I am grateful for:

My affirmation for the day:

Three things I will hold myself accountable
for today:

1.

2.

3.

Today I accomplished:

I am grateful for:

My affirmation for the day:

Three things I will hold myself accountable
for today:

1.

2.

3.

Today I accomplished:

ABOUT THE AUTHOR

Ahyiana Angel is the Founder of Mayzie Media a media company with content curated for women, and host of the Switch, Pivot or Quit podcast. She is affectionately known to many as the Chief Encourager. However, by design, Ahyiana is a creator. Creator of a buzz-worthy jewelry line featured by Vogue magazine and worn by Pop Icon Beyoncé, creator of a debut novel worthy of traditional publishing, and creator of a stellar career in publicity having worked with one of the top sports entertainment leagues, the National Basketball Association (NBA). Ultimately, one of her proudest accomplishments is creating an environment where women can consume thoughtful audio entertainment as a result of her positive energy, skill, and fearless attitude.

Ahyiana is a seasoned executor who eventually blocked out the world's ideas of success, quit her highly coveted position at the NBA, moved to London and traveled the world for a stint, then followed her passion in writing to find her purpose through encouragement. Mastering the art of note-worthy ideation and encouragement, Ahyiana taps into her zones of genius when speaking to audiences about her 4 Ps: publicity, publishing, personal development, and podcasting. With more than 15 years of professional business experience lending her knowledge in these areas, Ahyiana serves up real and relatable insight.

In addition to her extensive professional background, Ahyiana has a Bachelor of Science in Business Administration and Marketing from California State University, Long Beach.

Ahyiana and her work have been featured by Forbes, Black Enterprise, Essence, Career Contessa, and The Muse among others. Girlboss.com has highlighted the Switch, Pivot or Quit Podcast: "The 6 Best Podcasts To Listen To For Career Advice." Apple podcasts included it in the "Bold Women" featured collection.

Visit:

 @AhyianaAngel
@SwitchPivotorQuit

www.AhyianaAngel.com
www.SwitchPivotorQuit.com
www.MayzieMedia.com

Made in the USA
Lexington, KY
10 December 2019

58347344R00153